THE
CHRONOLOGY OF THE BIBLE
BY
Frank R. Klassen

PAINTINGS BY CLIFF JOHNSTON
NASHVILLE, TENNESSEE

Regal Publishers, inc.
961 Woodland Street, Nashville, Tennessee, 37206

KEY

All Scripture references in The Chronology of the Bible are taken from the King James Translation of the Bible.

AM, (ANNO MUNDI), in the year of the world AM Zero= 3975 B.C.

A.D., (ANNO DOMINI), in the year of our Lord begins page 50.

B.C., (BEFORE CHRIST), dates back from A.D. 1.

YOR, (YEAR OF ROME), (begins on page 41).

�as The heavy red line carries Christ's lineage, The Bloodline, from Adam.

―――――― The black line carries through the kings of Israel (pages 38-41).

▰▰▰ The heavy blue line carries the Levitical priestly lineage to Christ's birth.

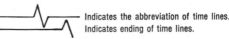

Indicates the abbreviation of time lines.
Indicates ending of time lines.

C, before a date means about or approximately.

INT. STD. BIBLE ENC. (ENC.), refers to International Standard Bible Encyclopedia. Scripture counts the first year and last year of a king's reign as full years (see bottom of page 38).

Judah's kings were buried in Jerusalem.

The accuracy of the Gregorian calendar brings the Bible dates through perfectly from Creation.

Use the datelines for an index. Events are usually found directly below their dates.

April is the first month of the year (Ex. 12:2, Esther 3:7) (page 23).

TABLE OF CONTENTS

PREFACE

God, the Master Architect, had a plan for Man before the world began. He provided the Savior before the foundation of the world (Matt. 25:34; Acts 15:18; Eph. 1:4; Rev. 13:8). Being a builder myself, I recognize the need of a plan (blueprint) for building. Using the King James Translation of the Bible, I have copied God's specifications. I have engineered the progression of dates and events, unfolding the panorama of the entire Bible. Building upon the foundation of Biblical dates, the plan of salvation has been brought into focus by means of The Chronology of the Bible. I have used dates, datelines, graphs, diagrams, tabulations, calendars, pictures, maps, and comments to accomplish this feat. Without my drafting and engineering experience, I could not have brought this tremendous production to completion.

Since I copied God's plan, He must receive all the credit for this accomplishment. He trained me for this undertaking; gave me an irresistible compulsion to keep going when the difficulties seemed insurmountable; and above all, gave me faith and unwavering confidence in His written Word. May His own purpose be brought about through this effort. When I met with my first difficulty, I realized it was God Who was giving me this supernatural drive; and without His guidance I could not have proceeded. After days of research, an impression came to me as real as if God had spoken audibly, "Are you going to believe the Bible, or believe what some commentators say about the Bible?" I immediately replied, "I'll believe the Bible, of course." In a few minutes, I had the answer from the Bible. Then came the assurance, "I helped you solve that problem. Now, go on to the next."

I discovered the date of Creation by accounting for each year from Creation to the anointing of Christ. From the year Adam was created, a mature man, to the baptism of Jesus, a mature man, is exactly 4,000 years. I chronicled the A. M. and B. C. dates on parallel datelines. The years of Rome began in 753 B.C. A third dateline, paralleling the others, carries the years of Rome, starting on page 41. Their dates synchronize. The rhythm of leap years is another factor to verify the progression of dates. Christ was born in 5 B.C. in a leap year. The next leap year is 1 B.C. The following leap year is A.D. 4, and so on. Luke recognizes the years of Rome (Luke 3:1; see diagram page 50, 63).

The Lineage to Christ faced extinction continually, but in each generation, God intervened to preserve the Royal Seed. This most famous family consisted of men who were sons of God through faith, as well as by blood. The mothers involved knew their responsibility. Eve recognized godly Seth. . . . For God, said she, hath appointed me another seed instead of Abel (Gen. 4:25; 5:3). Sarah was 90 years old when Isaac was born (Gen. 17:17; 21:5). Rebekah was blest to be the mother of thousands of millions (Gen. 24-60). Tamar was willing to give her life to preserve seed of Judah (Gen. 38). Ruth was to be like Rachel, and like Leah, which two did build the house of Israel (Ruth 4:11). Mary said to the angel, Behold the handmaid of the Lord; be it unto me according to thy word (Luke 1:38).

The calendar dating from Creation reveals God's pre-planned specifications for major events. Most of these occurred in April in the #7 and #13 calendar years. The death and resurrection of Jesus was pre-pictured by events in the Old Testament which took place the "selfsame" days (page 62). Jesus died when He was thirty-three years of age in A.D. 29, in the 29th jubilee year, during the famous sequence of dates and days, April 14 to 17. If Jesus had died eleven years earlier, when the selfsame days fell in A.D. 18, He would have been too young. If He had died six years later, when the selfsame days occurred in A.D. 35, He would have been too old pages(63, 64). The selfsame days in the #7 calendar year falling in A.D. 29 verify the year of Jesus' death. [By locating your calendar year (pages 63, 64), you can find the day of the week on which you were born.]

You will find The Chronology of the Bible an indispensable data-log. It is geared to supply Bible information to all ages, and to all faiths. It is a fresh comprehension of condensed Biblical knowledge; a remarkable learning system and fact-finder for self-education, as well as a manual for Bible instruction in schools. You will discover a wealth of Bible truths at your fingertips. This Chronology is a device to carry you dramatically through the Scriptures, and serve as a quick referral library as well. It lets the Bible speak for itself.

Study to shew thyself approved unto God, a workman that needeth not to be ashamed, rightly dividing the word of truth (2 Tim. 2:15).

Laguna Hills, California 92653
May 10, 1975

Frank R. Klassen

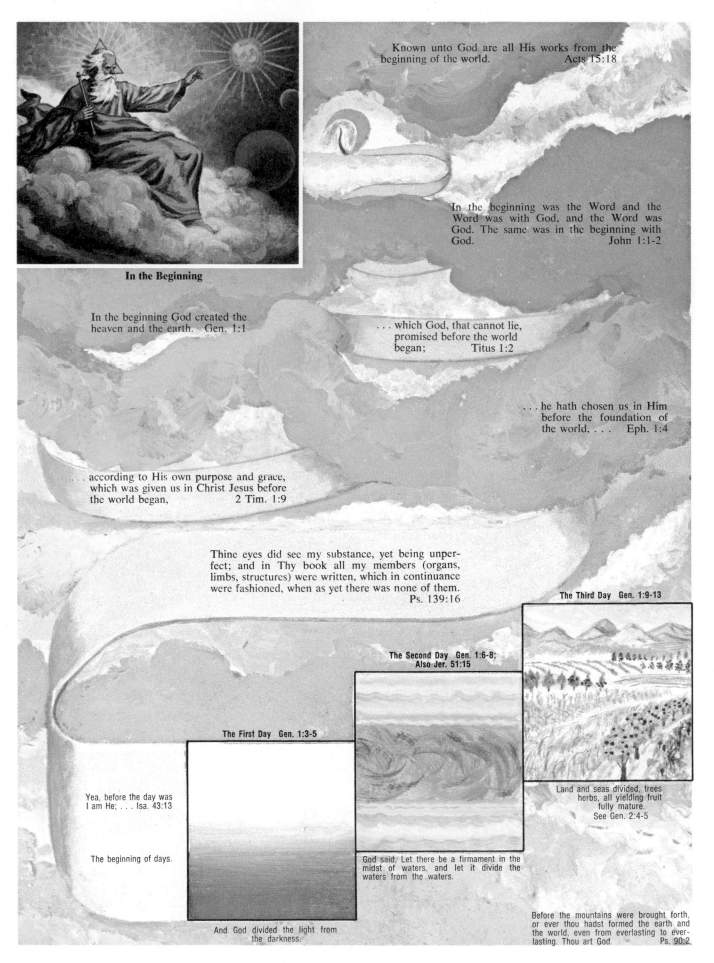

In the Beginning

Known unto God are all His works from the beginning of the world.   Acts 15:18

In the beginning was the Word and the Word was with God, and the Word was God. The same was in the beginning with God.   John 1:1-2

In the beginning God created the heaven and the earth.   Gen. 1:1

. . . which God, that cannot lie, promised before the world began;   Titus 1:2

. . . he hath chosen us in Him before the foundation of the world, . . .   Eph. 1:4

. . . according to His own purpose and grace, which was given us in Christ Jesus before the world began,   2 Tim. 1:9

Thine eyes did see my substance, yet being unperfect; and in Thy book all my members (organs, limbs, structures) were written, which in continuance were fashioned, when as yet there was none of them.   Ps. 139:16

The Third Day   Gen. 1:9-13

The Second Day   Gen. 1:6-8; Also Jer. 51:15

The First Day   Gen. 1:3-5

Yea, before the day was I am He; . . . Isa. 43:13

The beginning of days.

Land and seas divided, trees herbs, all yielding fruit fully mature. See Gen. 2:4-5

God said, Let there be a firmament in the midst of waters, and let it divide the waters from the waters.

And God divided the light from the darkness.

Before the mountains were brought forth, or ever thou hadst formed the earth and the world, even from everlasting to everlasting. Thou art God.   Ps. 90:2

Who hath measured the waters in the hollow of his hand, and meted out heaven with the span, and comprehended the dust of the earth in a measure, and weighed the mountains in scales, and the hills in a balance?   Isa. 40:12

God walking in the garden in the cool of the day: . . . Gen. 3:8

. . . God himself that formed the earth and made it; He hath established it, He created it not in vain, He formed it to be inhabited: I am the Lord; and there is none else.   Isa. 45:18

For ever, O Lord, Thy word is settled in heaven. Thy faithfulness is unto all generations: thou has established the earth, and it abideth. They continue this day according to thine ordinances: for all are thy servants.   Ps. 119:89-91

THE TEMPTATION

The Seventh Day Gen. 2:1-3

God blessed the seventh day and sanctified it; and He rested from all the work of His creation.

Adam and Eve's first day after creation was a sabbath.

SEE EX. 20:11.

And the Word was made flesh, and dwelt among us, . . .   John 1:14

The Messiah (Saviour) was promised. Gen. 3:15

THE CREATION

The Sixth Day Gen. 1:24-31 Gen. 2:4-25

God formed Man, beast, creatures, and creeping things from the dust of the earth. The green herb for their meat with every tree pleasant to the sight and for food. Adam named every beast, creature, and creeping thing. Eve was made from Adam's side. All creation was created mature, able to reproduce immediately.

The Fifth Day Gen. 1:20-23

The Fourth Day Gen. 1:14-19

The fowl of the air and the fish of the sea were created fully mature.

The rivers, seasons, floods and foundations were set. Job 28:10; Ps. 104

Let there be lights in the firmament for seasons, for days, and years: The greater light to rule the day, the lesser light to rule the night: He made the stars also.

God, . . . hath . . . spoken unto us, by His son, whom He hath appointed heir of all things, by whom also He made the worlds;   Heb. 1:1-2

By a perpetual decree the oceans and their bounds are established, until the day and night come to an end.
See Job 26:10-12
        Job 38:11
        Prov. 8:29
        Jer. 5:22
        Gen. 8:22

And hath made of one blood all nations of men for to dwell on all the face of the earth, and hath determined the times before appointed, and the bounds of their habitation;   Acts 17:26

B.C.	3975	3875	3775	3675	3575	3475	3375	3275
AM	0	100	200	300	400	500	600	700

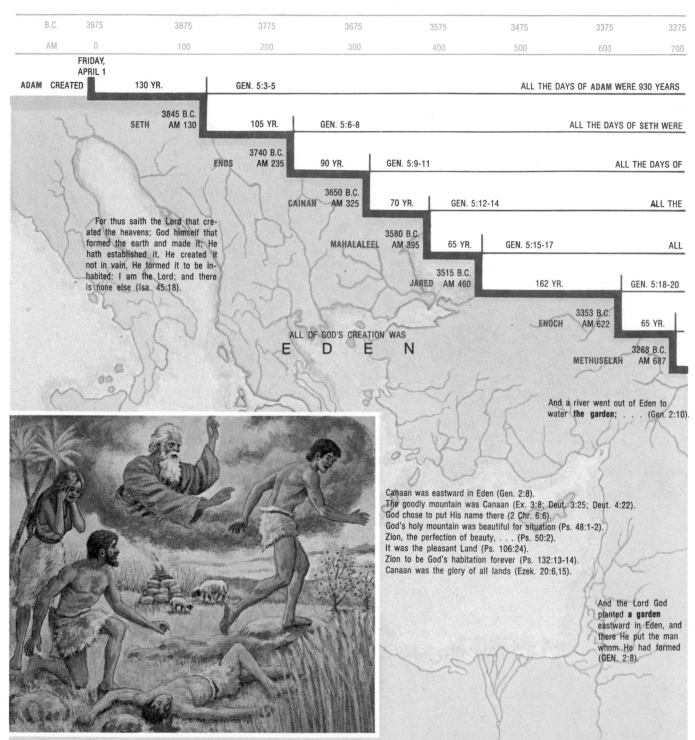

FRIDAY, APRIL 1

ADAM CREATED   130 YR.   GEN. 5:3-5   ALL THE DAYS OF ADAM WERE 930 YEARS

3845 B.C.
SETH   AM 130   105 YR.   GEN. 5:6-8   ALL THE DAYS OF SETH WERE

3740 B.C.
ENOS   AM 235   90 YR.   GEN. 5:9-11   ALL THE DAYS OF

3650 B.C.
CAINAN   AM 325   70 YR.   GEN. 5:12-14   ALL THE

3580 B.C.
MAHALALEEL   AM 395   65 YR.   GEN. 5:15-17   ALL

3515 B.C.
JARED   AM 460   162 YR.   GEN. 5:18-20

3353 B.C.
ENOCH   AM 622   65 YR.

3288 B.C.
METHUSELAH   AM 687

For thus saith the Lord that created the heavens; God himself that formed the earth and made it; He hath established it, He created it not in vain, He formed it to be inhabited: I am the Lord; and there is none else (Isa. 45:18).

ALL OF GOD'S CREATION WAS

E D E N

And a river went out of Eden to water the garden; . . . (Gen. 2:10).

Canaan was eastward in Eden (Gen. 2:8).
The goodly mountain was Canaan (Ex. 3:8; Deut. 3:25; Deut. 4:22).
God chose to put His name there (2 Chr. 6:6).
God's holy mountain was beautiful for situation (Ps. 48:1-2).
Zion, the perfection of beauty, . . . (Ps. 50:2).
It was the pleasant Land (Ps. 106:24).
Zion to be God's habitation forever (Ps. 132:13-14).
Canaan was the glory of all lands (Ezek. 20:6,15).

And the Lord God planted a garden eastward in Eden, and there He put the man whom He had formed (GEN. 2:8).

The giants were sons of the fugitive Cain. God rejected Cain and his offering because of sin. (Gen. 4:5,7). After murdering his brother Abel, God set a mark upon Cain to protect his life (Gen. 4:15). Since all Cain's descendants were giants, it is possible that his mark was an increase in his size, lest any finding him should kill him. He could be recognized at a distance. Noah was a just, or righteous man (Gen. 6:9). He was a son of God. (Read Luke 3:36-38; John 1:12; Rom. 8:14-16; 2 Cor. 6:18; Phil. 2:15; 1 John 3:1). Noah was perfect in his generations, so there was no giant blood in him. His first son was born twenty years after he started building the ark. Read Gen. 5:32; Gen. 6:3; Gen. 7:11-13 . Being unequally yoked together has always been a sin (2 Cor. 6:14). Ezra preserved the holy seed by separating their ungodly giantess wives and children from the sons of God. Read Ezra chapters 9 and 10 . Before the flood, all flesh had corrupted his way upon the earth (Gen. 6:13), because of believers marrying unbelievers. In Gen. 6:2, the sons of God were the believers. The daughters of men were the daughters of the unbelievers or giants. Read Ecc. 3:18-19; Eph. 3:5 . The mighty men of renown born to them received their might and size from their giantess mothers, and their renown from their intellectual fathers. This led to greater ungodliness (Gen. 6:1-7, 11-13). Ham, himself, was free of giant blood. Since he fathered the giants after the flood, his wife had to be a giantess. The sin in Ham's heart, causing him to sin against his father, came from his association with the giants. Noah called Ham Canaan (Cain) when he cursed him (Gen. 9:24-27). Cain was of that wicked one (1 John 3:10-12). God commanded Israel to utterly destroy the many nations of giants living in the Promised Land, when they came into the land to possess it. Read Deut. 7. See page 8 for Canaan's Land .

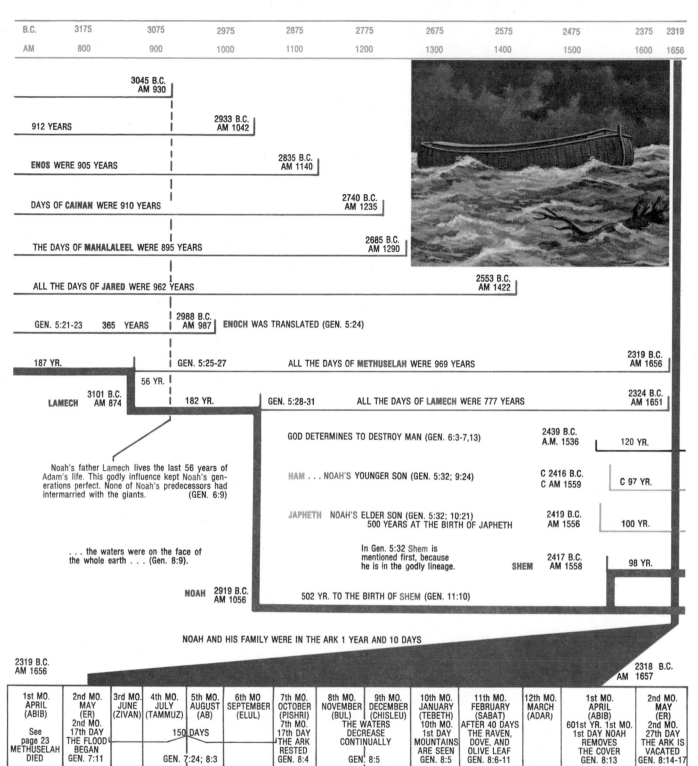

B.C.	3175	3075	2975	2875	2775	2675	2575	2475	2375	2319
AM	800	900	1000	1100	1200	1300	1400	1500	1600	1656

3045 B.C.
AM 930

912 YEARS

2933 B.C.
AM 1042

ENOS WERE 905 YEARS

2835 B.C.
AM 1140

DAYS OF CAINAN WERE 910 YEARS

2740 B.C.
AM 1235

THE DAYS OF MAHALALEEL WERE 895 YEARS

2685 B.C.
AM 1290

ALL THE DAYS OF JARED WERE 962 YEARS

2553 B.C.
AM 1422

GEN. 5:21-23   365   YEARS

2988 B.C.
AM 987   ENOCH WAS TRANSLATED (GEN. 5:24)

187 YR.   GEN. 5:25-27   ALL THE DAYS OF METHUSELAH WERE 969 YEARS

2319 B.C.
AM 1656

56 YR.

LAMECH   3101 B.C.
AM 874   182 YR.   GEN. 5:28-31   ALL THE DAYS OF LAMECH WERE 777 YEARS

2324 B.C.
AM 1651

Noah's father Lamech lives the last 56 years of Adam's life. This godly influence kept Noah's generations perfect. None of Noah's predecessors had intermarried with the giants.   (GEN. 6:9)

GOD DETERMINES TO DESTROY MAN (GEN. 6:3-7,13)   2439 B.C.
A.M. 1536   120 YR.

HAM . . . NOAH'S YOUNGER SON (GEN. 5:32; 9:24)   C 2416 B.C.
C AM 1559   C 97 YR.

JAPHETH   NOAH'S ELDER SON (GEN. 5:32; 10:21)
500 YEARS AT THE BIRTH OF JAPHETH   2419 B.C.
AM 1556   100 YR.

. . . the waters were on the face of the whole earth . . . (Gen. 8:9).

In Gen. 5:32 Shem is mentioned first, because he is in the godly lineage.   SHEM   2417 B.C.
AM 1558   98 YR.

NOAH   2919 B.C.
AM 1056   502 YR. TO THE BIRTH OF SHEM (GEN. 11:10)

NOAH AND HIS FAMILY WERE IN THE ARK 1 YEAR AND 10 DAYS

2319 B.C.
AM 1656

2318 B.C.
AM 1657

1st MO. APRIL (ABIB) See page 23 METHUSELAH DIED	2nd MO. MAY (ER) 2nd MO. 17th DAY THE FLOOD BEGAN GEN. 7:11	3rd MO. JUNE (ZIVAN)	4th MO. JULY (TAMMUZ) 150 DAYS	5th MO. AUGUST (AB)	6th MO. SEPTEMBER (ELUL) GEN. 7:24; 8:3	7th MO. OCTOBER (PISHRI) 7th MO. 17th DAY THE ARK RESTED GEN. 8:4	8th MO. NOVEMBER (BUL) THE WATERS DECREASE CONTINUALLY GEN. 8:5	9th MO. DECEMBER (CHISLEU)	10th MO. JANUARY (TEBETH) 10th MO. 1st DAY MOUNTAINS ARE SEEN GEN. 8:5	11th MO. FEBRUARY (SABAT) AFTER 40 DAYS THE RAVEN, DOVE, AND OLIVE LEAF GEN. 8:6-11	12th MO. MARCH (ADAR)	1st MO. APRIL (ABIB) 601st YR. 1st MO. 1st DAY NOAH REMOVES THE COVER GEN. 8:13	2nd MO. MAY (ER) 2nd MO. 27th DAY THE ARK IS VACATED GEN. 8:14-17

Ararat means "creation", "holy land", according to Young's Analytical Concordance of the Bible. Armenia never was the holy land of the Bible. The snow covered 16,945′ Mt. Ararat of Armenia has been so named "in comparatively modern times." (page 225 of The International Standard Bible Encyclopaedia). The mountains of Ararat in Gen. 8:4 could well have been the mountains of Jerusalem. Biblical facts favor this location. Their low altitude was the ideal climate for all life from the ark. The dove returned to Noah the same day with a plucked off olive leaf, possibly from the Mount of Olives (Gen. 8:11). The greatest altars were built to God in Jerusalem, where all the great sacrifices were made, including Abraham's sacrifice (Gen. 22:1-14), David's sacrifice (2 Sam. 24:15-25; 1 Chr. 21:18-30), on Ornan's threshing floor, which later became the Temple site, and Christ's offering of Himself (Heb. 7:27), on Calvary's altar (Luke 23:33). The Israelites were commanded to offer their burnt offerings in Jerusalem. Take heed to thyself that thou offer not thy burnt offerings in every place that thou seest: but in the place which the Lord shall choose in one of thy tribes, . . . (Deut. 12:13-14). That place was Jerusalem (1 Ki. 14:21; 2 Chr. 6:6; see page 37). The Rainbow Covenant with Noah could well have been made in Jerusalem, the central location from which Noah's sons overspread the whole earth (Gen. 9:19).

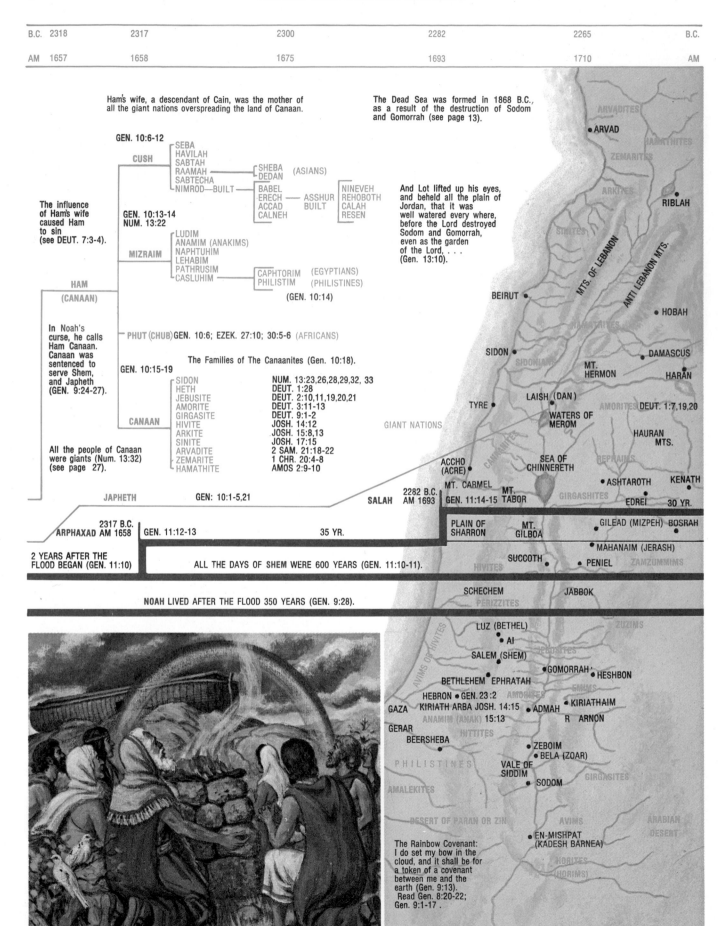

B.C.	2318	2317	2300	2282	2265	B.C.
AM	1657	1658	1675	1693	1710	AM

Ham's wife, a descendant of Cain, was the mother of all the giant nations overspreading the land of Canaan.

The Dead Sea was formed in 1868 B.C., as a result of the destruction of Sodom and Gomorrah (see page 13).

GEN. 10:6-12

CUSH
- SEBA
- HAVILAH
- SABTAH
- RAAMAH — SHEBA, DEDAN (ASIANS)
- SABTECHA
- NIMROD—BUILT — BABEL, ERECH, ACCAD, CALNEH — ASSHUR BUILT — NINEVEH, REHOBOTH, CALAH, RESEN

The influence of Ham's wife caused Ham to sin (see DEUT. 7:3-4).

And Lot lifted up his eyes, and beheld all the plain of Jordan, that it was well watered every where, before the Lord destroyed Sodom and Gomorrah, even as the garden of the Lord, . . . (Gen. 13:10).

GEN. 10:13-14
NUM. 13:22

MIZRAIM
- LUDIM
- ANAMIM (ANAKIMS)
- NAPHTUHIM
- LEHABIM
- PATHRUSIM — CAPHTORIM (EGYPTIANS)
- CASLUHIM — PHILISTIM (PHILISTINES)
(GEN. 10:14)

HAM (CANAAN)

In Noah's curse, he calls Ham Canaan. Canaan was sentenced to serve Shem, and Japheth (GEN. 9:24-27).

PHUT (CHUB) GEN. 10:6; EZEK. 27:10; 30:5-6 (AFRICANS)

The Families of The Canaanites (Gen. 10:18).

GEN. 10:15-19

CANAAN
- SIDON
- HETH
- JEBUSITE
- AMORITE
- GIRGASITE
- HIVITE
- ARKITE
- SINITE
- ARVADITE
- ZEMARITE
- HAMATHITE

NUM. 13:23,26,28,29,32, 33
DEUT. 1:28
DEUT. 2:10,11,19,20,21
DEUT. 3:11-13
DEUT. 9:1-2
JOSH. 14:12
JOSH. 15:8,13
JOSH. 17:15
2 SAM. 21:18-22
1 CHR. 20:4-8
AMOS 2:9-10

GIANT NATIONS

All the people of Canaan were giants (Num. 13:32) (see page 27).

JAPHETH   GEN: 10:1-5,21

SALAH   2282 B.C. AM 1693   GEN. 11:14-15

2317 B.C. ARPHAXAD AM 1658   GEN. 11:12-13   35 YR.

30 YR.

2 YEARS AFTER THE FLOOD BEGAN (GEN. 11:10).

ALL THE DAYS OF SHEM WERE 600 YEARS (GEN. 11:10-11).

NOAH LIVED AFTER THE FLOOD 350 YEARS (GEN. 9:28).

The Rainbow Covenant: I do set my bow in the cloud, and it shall be for a token of a covenant between me and the earth (Gen. 9:13). Read Gen. 8:20-22; Gen. 9:1-17 .

Map labels: ARVADITES, HAMATHITES, ARVAD, ZEMARITES, ARKITES, RIBLAH, SINITES, MTS. OF LEBANON, ANTI LEBANON MTS., BEIRUT, HOBAH, SIDON, SIDONIANS, DAMASCUS, MT. HERMON, HARAN, TYRE, LAISH (DAN), AMORITES DEUT. 1:7,19,20, WATERS OF MEROM, HAURAN MTS., CANAANITES, REPHAIMS, SEA OF CHINNERETH, ASHTAROTH, KENATH, ACCHO (ACRE), MT. CARMEL, MT. TABOR, GIRGASHITES, EDREI, PLAIN OF SHARRON, MT. GILBOA, GILEAD (MIZPEH), BOSRAH, MAHANAIM (JERASH), SUCCOTH, PENIEL, ZAMZUMMIMS, HIVITES, SCHECHEM, JABBOK, PERIZZITES, LUZ (BETHEL), ZUZIMS, AI, SALEM (SHEM), JEBUSITES, GOMORRAH, HESHBON, BETHLEHEM EPHRATAH, EMIMS, AMORITES, HEBRON GEN. 23:2, KIRIATHAIM, GAZA, KIRIATH ARBA JOSH. 14:15, ADMAH, R ARNON, ANAMIM (ANAK) 15:13, HITTITES, GERAR, BEERSHEBA, ZEBOIM, BELA (ZOAR), PHILISTINES, VALE OF SIDDIM, GIRGASHITES, SODOM, AMALEKITES, DESERT OF PARAN OR ZIN, AVIMS, ARABIAN DESERT, EN-MISHPAT (KADESH BARNEA), HORITES (HORIMS), WILDERNESS OF SHUR, AVIMS OR HIVITES

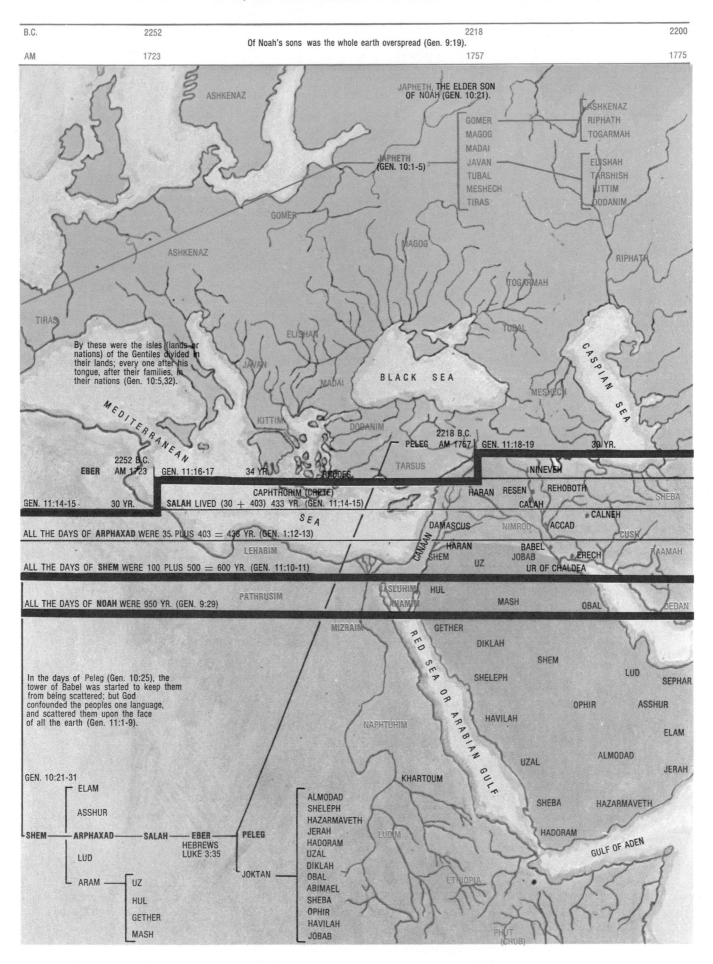

B.C.	2252		2218		2200
AM	1723		1757		1775

Of Noah's sons was the whole earth overspread (Gen. 9:19).

ASHKENAZ

JAPHETH, THE ELDER SON OF NOAH (GEN. 10:21).

JAPHETH (GEN. 10:1-5)

GOMER — ASHKENAZ / RIPHATH / TOGARMAH
MAGOG
MADAI
JAVAN — ELISHAH / TARSHISH / KITTIM / DODANIM
TUBAL
MESHECH
TIRAS

GOMER

ASHKENAZ

MAGOG

RIPHATH

TOGARMAH

TUBAL

TIRAS

ELISHAH

MESHECH

CASPIAN SEA

By these were the isles (lands or nations) of the Gentiles divided in their lands; every one after his tongue, after their families, in their nations (Gen. 10:5,32).

JAVAN

BLACK SEA

MEDITERRANEAN

MADAI

KITTIM

DODANIM

2218 B.C. PELEG AM 1757 GEN. 11:18-19 30 YR.

2252 B.C. EBER AM 1723 GEN. 11:16-17 34 YR.

RHODES

CAPHTHORIM (CRETE)

TARSUS

NINEVEH

HARAN RESEN REHOBOTH

SHEBA

GEN. 11:14-15 30 YR.

SALAH LIVED (30 + 403) 433 YR. (GEN. 11:14-15)

CALAH

SEA

CALNEH

DAMASCUS NIMROD ACCAD

ALL THE DAYS OF ARPHAXAD WERE 35. PLUS 403 = 438 YR. (GEN. 1:12-13)

CUSH

LEHABIM

CANAAN

HARAN

BABEL

RAAMAH

SHEM

UZ

JOBAB

ERECH

ALL THE DAYS OF SHEM WERE 100 PLUS 500 = 600 YR. (GEN. 11:10-11)

UR OF CHALDEA

CASLUHIM HUL

ALL THE DAYS OF NOAH WERE 950 YR. (GEN. 9:29)

PATHRUSIM

ANAMIM

MASH

OBAL

DEDAN

MIZRAIM

GETHER

RED SEA OR ARABIAN GULF

DIKLAH

SHEM

LUD

SEPHAR

In the days of Peleg (Gen. 10:25), the tower of Babel was started to keep them from being scattered; but God confounded the peoples one language, and scattered them upon the face of all the earth (Gen. 11:1-9).

SHELEPH

OPHIR

ASSHUR

NAPHTUHIM

HAVILAH

ELAM

UZAL

ALMODAD

JERAH

KHARTOUM

SHEBA

HAZARMAVETH

GEN. 10:21-31

ELAM

ASSHUR

SHEM — ARPHAXAD — SALAH — EBER — PELEG
HEBREWS
LUKE 3:35

LUD

ARAM — UZ / HUL / GETHER / MASH

JOKTAN — ALMODAD / SHELEPH / HAZARMAVETH / JERAH / HADORAM / UZAL / DIKLAH / OBAL / ABIMAEL / SHEBA / OPHIR / HAVILAH / JOBAB

HADORAM

LUDIM

ETHIOPIA

GULF OF ADEN

PHUT (CHUB)

B.C.	2188		2156		2126
AM	1787		1819		1849

And Abram and Nahor took them wives: the name of Abram's wife was Sarai; and the name of Nahor's wife was Milcah, the daughter of Haran, the father of Milcah, and the father of Iscah. But Sarai was barren; she had no child (Gen. 11:29-30).

And Terah took Abram his son, and Lot the son of Haran his son's son, and Sarai (his daughter) and daughter-in-law (Gen. 20:12), his son Abram's wife; and they went forth with them from Ur of the Chaldees, to go into the land of Canaan; and they came unto Haran, and dwelt there. And the days of Terah were two hundred and five years; and Terah died in Haran (Gen. 11:31-32).

A GATE OF HARAN TODAY

NAHOR 2126 B.C. AM 1849 GEN. 11:24-25

SERUG 2156 B.C. AM 1819 GEN. 11:22-23   30 YR.   200 YR.

REU 2188 B.C. AM 1787 GEN. 11:20-21   32 YR.   GEN. 11:20-21   REU   32 PLUS 207 = 239 YR.

30 YR.   GEN. 11:18-19   ALL THE DAYS OF **PELEG** WERE 30 PLUS 209 = 239 YR.

GEN. 11:16-17   ALL THE DAYS OF **EBER** WERE 34 PLUS 430 = 464 YR.

GEN. 11:14-15   ALL THE DAYS OF **SALAH** WERE 30 PLUS 403 = 433 YR.

GEN. 11:12-13   ALL THE DAYS OF **ARPHAXAD** WERE 35 PLUS 403 = 438 YR.

GEN. 11:10-11   **SHEM**

GEN. 9:28-29   **NOAH**

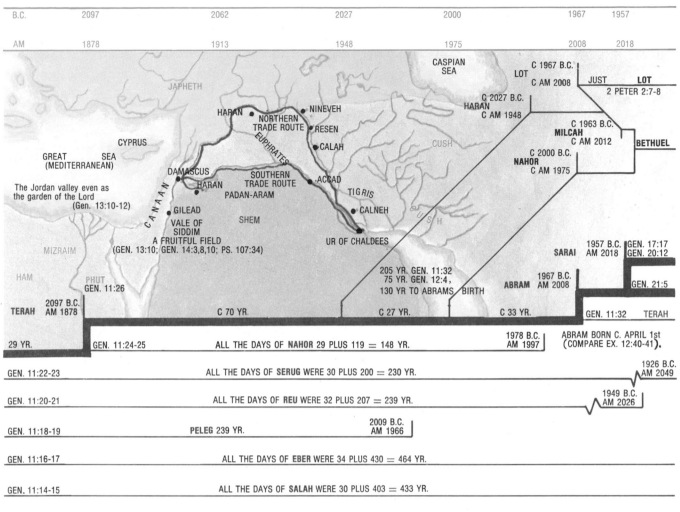

B.C.	2097	2062	2027	2000	1967	1957
AM	1878	1913	1948	1975	2008	2018

CASPIAN SEA

LOT
C 1967 B.C.
C AM 2008 — JUST **LOT**
2 PETER 2:7-8

HARAN
C 2027 B.C.
C AM 1948

JAPHETH

NINEVEH
HARAN
NORTHERN TRADE ROUTE
RESEN

MILCAH
C 1963 B.C.
C AM 2012 — **BETHUEL**

CYPRUS

EUPHRATES

CALAH

CUSH

NAHOR
C 2000 B.C.
C AM 1975

GREAT SEA (MEDITERRANEAN)

DAMASCUS
SOUTHERN TRADE ROUTE
ACCAD

The Jordan valley even as the garden of the Lord (Gen. 13:10-12)

HARAN
PADAN-ARAM

TIGRIS

GILEAD
VALE OF SIDDIM
A FRUITFUL FIELD
(GEN. 13:10; GEN. 14:3,8,10; PS. 107:34)

SHEM

CALNEH

UR OF CHALDEES

SARAI
1957 B.C.
AM 2018 — GEN. 17:17
GEN. 20:12

MIZRAIM

205 YR. GEN. 11:32
75 YR. GEN. 12:4,
130 YR TO ABRAMS BIRTH

ABRAM
1967 B.C.
AM 2008

GEN. 21:5

HAM

PHUT
GEN. 11:26

TERAH
2097 B.C.
AM 1878

C 70 YR.

C 27 YR.

C 33 YR.

GEN. 11:32 TERAH

29 YR.

GEN. 11:24-25 ALL THE DAYS OF **NAHOR** 29 PLUS 119 = 148 YR.

1978 B.C.
AM 1997

ABRAM BORN C. APRIL 1st
(COMPARE EX. 12:40-41).

GEN. 11:22-23 ALL THE DAYS OF **SERUG** WERE 30 PLUS 200 = 230 YR.

1926 B.C.
AM 2049

GEN. 11:20-21 ALL THE DAYS OF **REU** WERE 32 PLUS 207 = 239 YR.

1949 B.C.
AM 2026

GEN. 11:18-19 **PELEG** 239 YR.

2009 B.C.
AM 1966

GEN. 11:16-17 ALL THE DAYS OF **EBER** WERE 34 PLUS 430 = 464 YR.

GEN. 11:14-15 ALL THE DAYS OF **SALAH** WERE 30 PLUS 403 = 433 YR.

GEN. 11:12-13 ALL THE DAYS OF **ARPHAXAD** WERE 35 PLUS 403 = 438 YR.

GEN. 11:10-11 **SHEM**

1969 B.C.
AM 2006

Noah's total days were 950 years (Gen. 9:28-29). He lived to within 2 years of the birth of Abram.

Assuming Abram was 40 years old when they left the Ur of Chaldees other members of the family would be about:

Salah	355 years old
Eber	325 years old
Serug	229 years old
Terah	170 years old
Abram	40 years old
Sarai	30 years old
Lot	40 years old
Milcah	25 years old

B.C.

AM

| | | 1892 | 1889 |
| | | 2083 | 2086 |

				C 1889 B.C.	
JUST LOT 2 PETER 2:7-8				C AM 2086	**LOT**
JUST MEANS RIGHTEOUS (2 PETER 2:8).					
LOT CHOSE THE WELL WATERED PLAIN OF JORDAN (GEN. 13:10).					

BETHUEL

·Abram dwelled in the land of Canaan, and Lot dwelled in the cities of the plain, and pitched his tent toward Sodom (Gen. 13:12).

GEN. 17:17		**SARAH**		90 YR.
(GEN. 12:4) 75 YR. WHEN HE LEFT HARAN	**ABRAM**		1892 B.C. AM 2083	GEN. 16 GEN. 16:16
(GEN. 11:32) **TERAH**	205 YR.		1892 B.C. AM 2083	

The beginning of the 430-year sojourn was started in Abraham's 75th year (Gen. 12:1-8; Ex. 12:40-41; Acts 7:1-7; Heb. 11:8-9).

GEN. 11:16-17	ALL THE DAYS OF **EBER** WERE 464 YR.
GEN. 11:14-15	ALL THE DAYS OF **SALAH** WERE 433 YR.
GEN. 11:12-13	ALL THE DAYS OF **ARPHAXAD** WERE 438 YR.
GEN. 11:10-11	ALL THE DAYS OF **SHEM (MELCHIZEDEK)** WERE 600 YR.

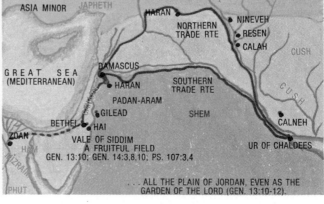

Abram entered Canaan April 15, 1892 B.C. He was 75. His father, Terah, had just died at 205. Terah had brought his family from Ur, along the southern trade route, settling at the Haran just S. E. of Damascus. Abram took a servant from nearby Damascus, whose son, Eliezer, born in Abram's house, became Abram's steward (Gen. 15:2-3). One hundred and seventy-nine years later, it took Jacob 10 days to drive his flocks and herds with young from Haran to Mt. Gilead (Gen. 31:22-23; 33-13). The Haran on the northern route, would have taken much longer than a 10-day journey.

ASIA MINOR   JAPHETH   HARAN   NINEVEH   NORTHERN TRADE RTE   RESEN   CALAH   CUSH

GREAT SEA (MEDITERRANEAN)   DAMASCUS   HARAN   SOUTHERN TRADE RTE   SHEM   CUSH

PADAN-ARAM   GILEAD   CALNEH

BETHEL   HAI   SHEM

ZOAN   VALE OF SIDDIM   A FRUITFUL FIELD   GEN. 13:10; GEN. 14:3,8,10; PS. 107:3,4   UR OF CHALDEES

HAM   MIZRAIM

PHUT   ... ALL THE PLAIN OF JORDAN, EVEN AS THE GARDEN OF THE LORD (GEN. 13:10-12).

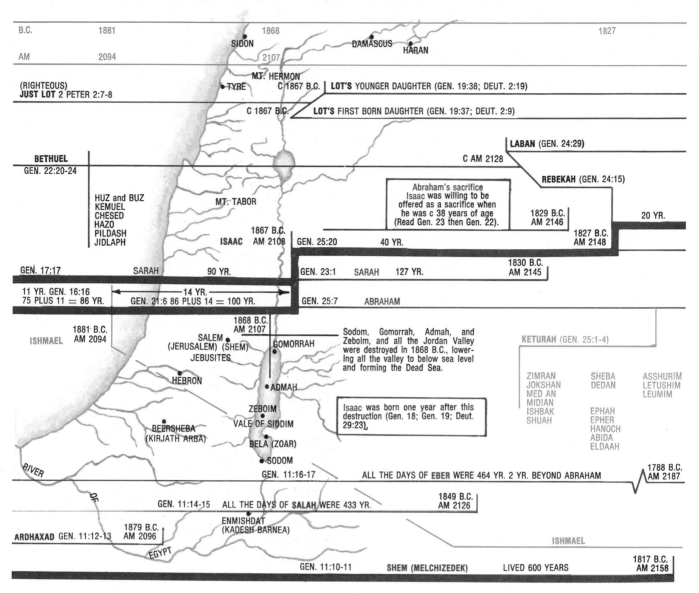

| B.C. | 1881 | | 1868 | | | 1827 |
| AM | 2094 | | 2107 | | | |

SIDON

DAMASCUS HARAN

MT. HERMON

(RIGHTEOUS)
JUST LOT 2 PETER 2:7-8   TYRE   C 1867 B.C.   **LOT'S** YOUNGER DAUGHTER (GEN. 19:38; DEUT. 2:19)

C 1867 B.C.   **LOT'S** FIRST BORN DAUGHTER (GEN. 19:37; DEUT. 2:9)

LABAN (GEN. 24:29)

BETHUEL   C AM 2128
GEN. 22:20-24

REBEKAH (GEN. 24:15)

HUZ and BUZ   MT. TABOR   Abraham's sacrifice
KEMUEL   Isaac was willing to be
CHESED   offered as a sacrifice when   1829 B.C.   20 YR.
HAZO   he was c 38 years of age   AM 2146
PILDASH   1867 B.C.   (Read Gen. 23 then Gen. 22).
JIDLAPH   **ISAAC** AM 2108   GEN. 25:20   40 YR.   1827 B.C.
                                                                                                     AM 2148
GEN. 17:17   SARAH   90 YR.   GEN. 23:1   SARAH   127 YR.   1830 B.C.
                                                                                     AM 2145
11 YR. GEN. 16:16   ◄——————— 14 YR. ———————►
75 PLUS 11 = 86 YR. GEN. 21:6 86 PLUS 14 = 100 YR.   GEN. 25:7   **ABRAHAM**

                                    1868 B.C.
                                    AM 2107
ISHMAEL 1881 B.C.   SALEM   Sodom, Gomorrah, Admah, and   **KETURAH** (GEN. 25:1-4)
             AM 2094   (JERUSALEM) (SHEM) GOMORRAH   Zeboim, and all the Jordan Valley
                        JEBUSITES   were destroyed in 1868 B.C., lower-
                                           ing all the valley to below sea level   ZIMRAN   SHEBA   ASSHURIM
            HEBRON   and forming the Dead Sea.   JOKSHAN   DEDAN   LETUSHIM
                                                                                    MED AN   LEUMIM
                        ADMAH   MIDIAN
                                           Isaac was born one year after this   ISHBAK   EPHAH
                        ZEBOIM   destruction (Gen. 18; Gen. 19; Deut.   SHUAH   EPHER
         BEERSHEBA   VALE OF SIDDIM   29:23).   HANOCH
        (KIRJATH ARBA)   ABIDA
                        BELA (ZOAR)   ELDAAH
                        SODOM
RIVER   GEN. 11:16-17   ALL THE DAYS OF **EBER** WERE 464 YR. 2 YR. BEYOND ABRAHAM   1788 B.C.
                                                                                                            AM 2187
OF
                                                          1849 B.C.
      GEN. 11:14-15   ALL THE DAYS OF **SALAH** WERE 433 YR.   AM 2126
             1879 B.C. ENMISHDAT
ARDHAXAD GEN. 11:12-13 AM 2096 (KADESH BARNEA)   **ISHMAEL**
EGYPT
                                                                                                            1817 B.C.
             GEN. 11:10-11   **SHEM (MELCHIZEDEK)**   LIVED 600 YEARS   AM 2158

Melchizedek (Melchisedec) was the priestly name for Shem. He pre-pictured Christ. The Lord sware and will not repent, "Thou art a priest forever after the order of Melchizedek", (Ps. 110:4; Heb. 5:6,10; 6:20; 7:17,21). Shem, an antediluvian whose righteousness allowed him to outlive two great judgments, lived 502 years after the Flood (Gen. 11:10-11; page 7), and 52 years after the destruction of Sodom and Gomorrah, and 150 years of Abraham's life (see above). At the time Abraham paid tithes to him, Shem was the oldest man living upon the earth. He was priest of the most high God (Gen. 14:18; Heb. 7:1). Consider how great this man was, unto whom even the Patriarch Abraham gave the tenth of the spoils (Heb. 7:4). Shem named his city Shem (Jerusalem) after himself (Gen. 14:18; Ps. 76:2; Heb. 7:1). The king's dale is at Jerusalem, where Absalom's tomb still stands (Gen. 14:17; 2 Sam. 18:18).

	1. King of righteousness (Heb. 7:2).
Melchizedek's titles	2. King of Salem (peace) (Jerusalem) (Gen. 14:18; Heb. 1:2; 7:2).
are also	3. Priest of the most high God (Gen. 14:18; Heb. 7:1) Melchizedek (Shem) was the only high priest to be King
Christ's titles:	of Jerusalem. He pre-pictured Christ, our high priest, who will be King of Jerusalem when He returns to this earth.

"Without father, without mother," (Heb. 7:3) means "without Levitical parents," as explained in (Heb. 7:5-6) Jesus did not descend from the tribe of Levi either. He sprang from Judah, who never served as a high priest (Heb. 7:14). Shem's parents were Noah and his wife who lived before the Levitical priesthood was established (pages 7,24). Christ's and Melchizedek's (Shem's) priesthoods are alike in three points:

1. Neither sprang from Levi (Heb. 7:2)
2. Each has a continuing and unchangeable priesthood (Heb. 7:3,8,24)
3. Their priesthood's were not made by a carnal commandment, as were the Levitical priests; but appointed of God, after the power of an endless life (Termless) (Heb. 7:15-21)

Because the Levitical priesthood was changed, the law, also, was changed to a better testament (Heb. 7:15-22; 8:6-8).

B.C.	1807		1775
AM	2168		2200

LOT'S YOUNGER DAUGHTER WAS THE GENETRIX OF NAAMAH, THE AMMONITESS (GEN. 19:38; DEUT. 2:19; 1 KI. 14:21).

LOT'S FIRST-BORN WAS THE GENETRIX OF RUTH, THE MOABITESS (GEN. 19:37; DEUT. 2:9; RUTH 4:5).

FOUR OF **LABAN'S** DAUGHTERS BECOME THE MOTHERS OF PATRIARCHS (GEN. 31:26,43)

ESAU	1807 B.C. AM 2168	(GEN. 25:26)	WHOM GOD HATED (MAL. 1:3; ROM. 9:13), (Esau's posterity below).
JACOB	1807 B.C. AM 2168	(GEN. 25:26)	JACOB WHOM GOD LOVED (PS. 47:4; MAL. 1:2; ROM. 9:13). Jacob was 77 years old when he departed for Haran for a wife.

ALL THE DAYS OF ISAAC WERE 180 YEARS (GEN. 35:28).

Jacob was born in 1807 B.C., when Isaac was 60 years old.

ABRAHAM	175 YEARS	1792 B.C. AM 2183

Jacob means: to follow, to heel, to succeed, to take the place of another, as God rewardeth, or God hath given (Gen. 25:19-28). (International Standard Bible Encyclopedia page 1549 .

JACOB'S AGE DETERMINED		JACOB'S AGE DETERMINED	
Gen. 47:28 Jacob lived to be . . . . .147 yr. old		Gen. 41:46 Joseph was now . . . . 30 yr. old	
Gen. 47:28 Jacob dwelt in Egypt . . . . . . 17 yr.		Gen. 41:47 Seven years of plenty . . . . . . 7 yr.	
Gen. 47: 9 Jacob says I am . . . . .130 yr. old		Gen. 45: 6 Jacob came to Egypt after . . 2 yr.	
Gen. 45: 6 After two years of famine . . 2 yr.		Total . . 39 yr.	
Jacob was now . . . . .128 yr. old		Gen. 47:28 Jacob dwelt in Egypt . . . . . . 17 yr.	
Gen. 41:47 Seven years of plenty . . . . . . 7 yr.		Joseph was now . . . . 56 yr. old	
Jacob was now . . . . .121 yr. old		Gen. 47:28 Jacob died when he was . . .147 yr. old	
Gen. 41:46 Joseph was . . . . 30 yr. old		Minus Joseph's age . . . . 56 yr.	
Jacob at Joseph's birth . . . . . 91 yr. old		Jacob at Joseph's birth . . . . . 91 yr. old	
11 Patriarchs and Dinah are born in . . . . . . 7 yr.		Gen. 29:27 Yet seven other years . . . . . . 7 yr.	
Jacob at Reuben's birth . . . . 84 yr. old		Jacob at Reuben's birth . . . . 84 yr. old	
Gen. 29:20 Jacob labors for Rachel . . . . 7 yr.		Gen. 29:20 Jacob labors for Rachel . . . . 7 yr.	
Jacob went to Padan-aram when he was . . . 77 yr. old		Jacob went to Padan-aram when he was . . 77 yr. old	

ISHMAEL GEN. 25:12-18   LIVED 137 YEARS   1744 B.C. AM 2231

GEN. 36:2 ZIBEON THE HIVITE GIANT

ANAH

JACOB AND ESAU ARE NOW 77 YEARS OF AGE 1730 B.C. AM 2245

BEERI THE GIANT HITTITE'S DAUGHTER **JUDITH** GEN 26:34

AHOLIBAMAH GEN. 36:14,18

[**JEUSH** **JAALAM** 1 CHR. 1:35 **KORAH**

ESAU	1767 B.C. AM 2208

ESAU WAS 40 YR. OLD GEN. 26:34

WHEN ESAU WAS 77 YEARS OF AGE HE TOOK MAHALATH, DAUGHTER OF ISHMAEL, TO WIFE TO TRY TO PLEASE ISAAC AND REBEKAK (GEN. 28:1-9). CALLED BASHEMATH (GEN. 36:3).

TIMNA — **AMALEK** **KORAH**
THE TWIN SISTER OF LOTAN THE HORITE GEN. 36:12,16,20,22

ELON THE GIANT HITTITE'S DAUGHTER **BASHEMATH** GEN. 26:34 **(ADAH)** GEN. 36:2

ELIPHAZ — GEN. 36:10-16 [**TEMAN** **OMAR** **ZEPHO** **GATAM** **KENAZ**

BASHEMATH ——— **REUEL** ——— GEN. 36:13 / 1 CHR. 1:37 [NAHATH ZERAH SHAMMAH MIZZAH

TWIN SISTER OF NEBAJOTH GEN. 28:9; GEN. 36:3,4
MAHALATH
KEDAR
ADBEEL
MIBSAM
MISHMA
DUMAH
MASSA
HADAR
TEMA
JETUR
NAPHISH
KEDEMAH

Abraham, through Ishmael and Esau, became the progenitor of Moses' father-in-law, known as Reuel, Jethro, the priest of Midian, Raguel, the Kenite, and Hobab (see below).
Jethro gives Moses the plan to judge all Israel (Ex. 18:13-27). (page 22).

Moses' father-in-law was known as:
Reuel in Gen. 36:4,10,13,17;
Ex. 2:18; 1 Chr. 1:35,37

Jethro, the priest of Midian in Ex. 3:1; Ex. 4:18; Ex. 18:1,2,5,6,9, 10, 12

Raguel in Num. 10:29

Hobab in Jud. 4-11

The Kenite in Jud. 1:16; Jud. 4:11, 17

The Kenites, Moses' in-laws, become part of Judah's tribe in the inheritance (see Num. 10:29-32; Jud. 1:16); (See **Map** Page 31).

B.C. 1730
AM 2245

Esau despised his birthright. Willingly, he sold it to Jacob.
... as a prince hast thou power with God . . . (Gen. 32:28; Gen. 35:10; Compare Rom. 9:10-12).

1730
2245

LOT'S

LOT'S

LABAN'S

JACOB
(ISRAEL)

ISAAC

LOT'S

LOT'S

LABAN'S

JACOB

ISAAC

JACOB DREAMS AT BETHEL (GEN. 28:10-22)

Jacob have I loved, but Esau have I hated (Mal. 1:2,3 ; Rom. 9:13). The struggle between Jacob and Esau began in Rebekah's womb before their birth. When she brought her problem to the Lord, God told her, "Two nations are in thy womb, and two manner of people shall be separated from thy bowels; and the one people shall be stronger than the other people; and the elder shall serve the younger" (Gen. 25:23). At birth, his strength was evident when Jacob grasped Esau's heel (Hosea 12:3; Gen. 25:26). Esau was a fornicator, and a profane person (Heb. 12:16). Jacob was a plain man (Gen. 25:27), which means he was godly, honest, righteous, faithful, law-abiding, and trustworthy. Jacob had proven himself before God named him Israel (a prince of God) (Gen. 32:28). When Jacob's mother insisted that he deceive his father, Isaac, Jacob objected lest he seem to be a deceiver (Gen. 27:12). Rebekah, certain of God's will, said, "Upon me be thy curse, only obey my voice, . . ." (Gen. 27:13). Jacob obtained the birthright and blessing in God's providence (Gen. 25:29-34; Gen. chapter 27). It was needful to thwart Isaac's scheme in order to preserve the godly link in the lineage (blood line) to Christ. Isaac did not care about God's will that the elder should serve the younger. Isaac "trembled very exceedingly", when he realized that he had nearly thwarted God's plan (Gen. 27:33). He, then, listened to Rebekah's plea that Jacob must go to Padan-aram to take a wife from his uncle Laban's daughters (Gen. 27:41-46; Gen. 28:1,2). Jacob obeyed (Gen. 28:7). God appeared to Jacob in a dream, at Bethel, and re-established the covenant He had made with Abraham and Isaac. God, thus, approved godly Jacob to be the next man in the lineage (blood line) to Christ (Gen. 28:12-15). God blest Jacob in spite of the injustices and privations he endured at the hands of Laban. Laban admitted that the Lord had blest him for Jacob's sake (Gen. 30:27). Before Jacob served for his stock, he warned Laban, "So shall my righteousness answer for me in time to come, when it shall come for my hire before thy face: . . ." (Gen. 30:33). In a dream, God gave Jacob the method to use to produce his variety of cattle (Gen. 31:7-12). Jacob's wives agreed that all the riches, which God had taken from their father, was rightfully theirs (Gen. 31:14-16). Their journey from Haran to Gilead with tender children, and with the flocks and herds with young (Gen. 33:13), took ten days (Gen. 31:22-23; page 12).

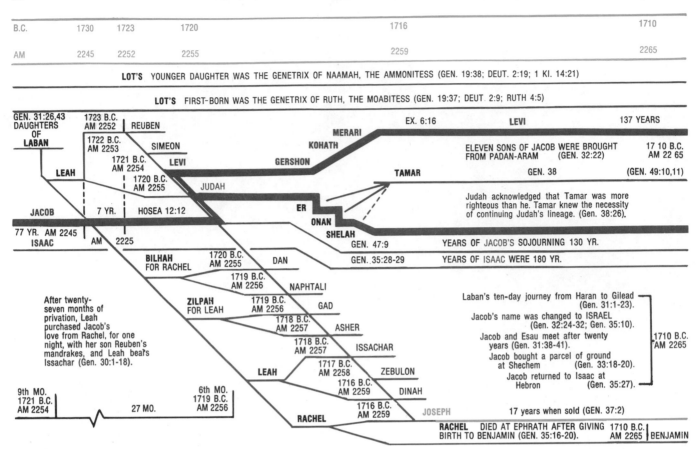

After serving seven years for Rachel, Laban gave Jacob Leah instead, saying that the younger should not be given before the first born. He told Jacob to fulfill Leah's week (her wedding week of seven days), and he would give him Rachel also, for whom he should work seven more years (Gen. 29:26-30). Jacob received both wives seven days apart. God saw that Rachel was loved, and Leah was hated, so let Leah bear children (Gen. 29:31). Leah bore six of the patriarchs (Gen. 29:31-35; Gen. 30:18,19). Because she was barren, Rachel gave her maid, Bilhah, to Jacob to wife. Bilhah bore two sons for Rachel. Then because Leah had left bearing, she gave Jacob her maid, Zilpah, who bore two sons for Leah (Gen. 30:1-12). Then Leah bore two more sons and a daughter (Gen. 30:16-21). Rachel, when she was fully paid for, bore Joseph. Six years later, she died at the birth of Benjamin (Gen. 36:16-19).

JACOB SERVED LABAN TWENTY YEARS, FROM 77 YEARS OF AGE UNTIL HE WAS 97 YEARS OF AGE (Gen. 31:38-41).

SEVEN YEARS FOR LEAH	SEVEN YEARS FOR RACHEL	SIX YEARS FOR THE CATTLE
Jacob served seven years for Rachel, but Laban gave him Leah instead. After Leah's wedding week of seven days, Jacob received Rachel also, with the promise that he would serve seven more years (Gen. 29:27-29).	During this second seven year period, eleven of the patriarchs and Dinah were born to Laban's daughters (Gen. 31:43,50). At the end of the fourteen years, when Rachel was fully paid for, she bore Joseph, her first born child.	Jacob served six years for his cattle (Gen. 31:41). When they left Haran for Canaan, Rachel was heavy with child. Rachel's son Benjamin was born near Bethlehem. Dinah was six years old when they reached Canaan.
1730 B.C. AM 2245	1723 B.C. AM 2252	1716 B.C. AM 2259	1710 B.C. AM 2265

BIRTH CALENDAR OF THE PATRIARCHS

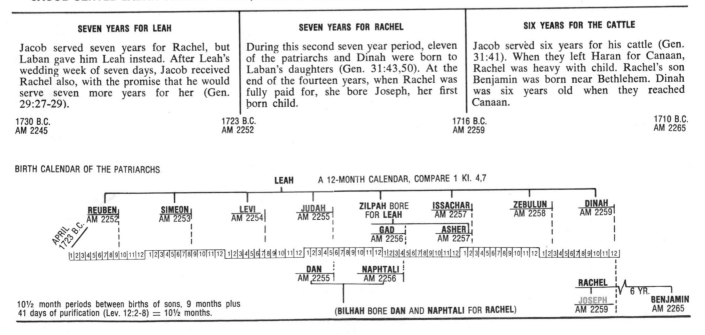

10½ month periods between births of sons, 9 months plus 41 days of purification (Lev. 12:2-8) = 10½ months.

(BILHAH BORE DAN AND NAPHTALI FOR RACHEL)

| B.C. | 1710 | | 1710 |
| AM | 2265 | | 2265 |

Jacob's name was changed to Israel at Peniel (Gen. 24-32; 1710 B.C.).

LOT'S — YOUNGER DAUGHTER BORE BENAMMI, THE FATHER OF THE AMMONITES (GEN. 19:38; 1 KI. 14:21)

LOT'S — FIRST-BORN DAUGHTER BORE MOAB, THE FATHER OF THE MOABITES (GEN. 19:37; RUTH 4:5)

LEVI — FATHER OF THE LEVITICAL PRIESTLY LINE LIVED 137 YEARS (EX. 6:16)

TAMAR — Both Judah and Tamar knew that Shiloh (the Saviour) would come through Judah. "The sceptre shall not depart from Judah, . . . until Shiloh come;" (Gen. 49:10; 1 Chr. 5:2). At the risk of being burned, Tamar played the harlot to preserve Judah's seed. When she proved

JUDAH — him the father of her child, he said she was more righteous than he, because she was more concerned about the preservation of his seed than he was (Gen. 38:26). Tamar is given worthy mention in Ruth 4:12: is a mother in Christ's lineage (Matt. 1:3).

JACOB'S SOJOURNING (PILGRIMAGE) (STRANGER) IN THE LAND OF CANAAN (GEN. 28:4; GEN. 47:9).

ALL THE DAYS OF **ISAAC** WERE 180 YEARS (GEN. 35:28-29)

JOSEPH

BENJAMIN

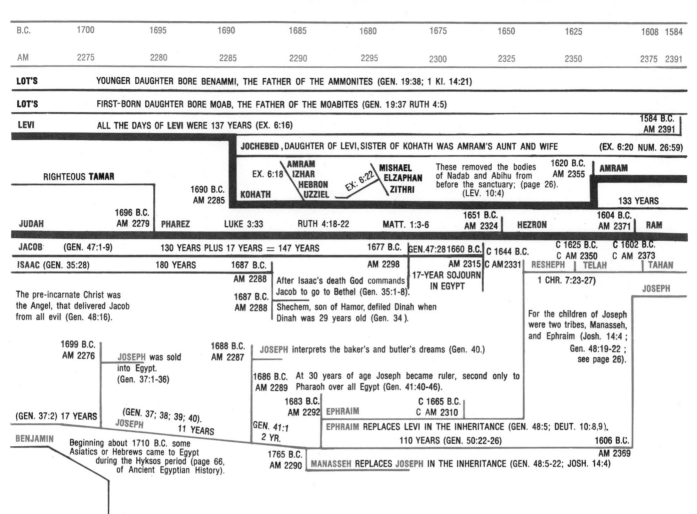

THE 70 SOULS WHICH CAME INTO EGYPT (GEN. 46:7-27; DEUT. 10:22)

18

B.C.	1700	1695	1690	1685	1680	1675	1650	1625	1608	1584
AM	2275	2280	2285	2290	2295	2300	2325	2350	2375	2391

LOT'S YOUNGER DAUGHTER BORE BENAMMI, THE FATHER OF THE AMMONITES (GEN. 19:38; 1 KI. 14:21)

LOT'S FIRST-BORN DAUGHTER BORE MOAB, THE FATHER OF THE MOABITES (GEN. 19:37 RUTH 4:5)

LEVI ALL THE DAYS OF LEVI WERE 137 YEARS (EX. 6:16)   1584 B.C. AM 2391

JOCHEBED, DAUGHTER OF LEVI, SISTER OF KOHATH WAS AMRAM'S AUNT AND WIFE   (EX. 6:20 NUM. 26:59)

RIGHTEOUS TAMAR

EX. 6:18 **AMRAM IZHAR HEBRON UZZIEL** KOHATH   EX. 6:22   **MISHAEL ELZAPHAN ZITHRI**   These removed the bodies of Nadab and Abihu from before the sanctuary; (page 26). (LEV. 10:4).   1620 B.C. AM 2355   **AMRAM**

1690 B.C. AM 2285   133 YEARS

JUDAH   1696 B.C. AM 2279   **PHAREZ**   LUKE 3:33   RUTH 4:18-22   MATT. 1:3-6   1651 B.C. AM 2324   **HEZRON**   1604 B.C. AM 2371   **RAM**

JACOB (GEN. 47:1-9)   130 YEARS PLUS 17 YEARS = 147 YEARS   1677 B.C.   GEN. 47:28 1660 B.C.   C 1644 B.C.   C 1625 B.C. C AM 2350   C 1602 B.C. C AM 2373

ISAAC (GEN. 35:28)   180 YEARS   1687 B.C.   AM 2298   AM 2315 C AM2331   **RESHEPH** | **TELAH**   **TAHAN**

AM 2288   After Isaac's death God commands Jacob to go to Bethel (Gen. 35:1-8).   17-YEAR SOJOURN IN EGYPT   1 CHR. 7:23-27)

The pre-incarnate Christ was the Angel, that delivered Jacob from all evil (Gen. 48:16).   1687 B.C. AM 2288   Shechem, son of Hamor, defiled Dinah when Dinah was 29 years old (Gen. 34).   **JOSEPH**

For the children of Joseph were two tribes, Manasseh, and Ephraim (Josh. 14:4; Gen. 48:19-22; see page 26).

1699 B.C. AM 2276   **JOSEPH** was sold into Egypt. (Gen. 37:1-36)   1688 B.C. AM 2287   **JOSEPH** interprets the baker's and butler's dreams (Gen. 40.)

1686 B.C. AM 2289   At 30 years of age Joseph became ruler, second only to Pharaoh over all Egypt (Gen. 41:40-46).

1683 B.C. AM 2292   **EPHRAIM**   C 1665 B.C. C AM 2310

(GEN. 37:2) 17 YEARS   (GEN. 37; 38; 39; 40). **JOSEPH** 11 YEARS   GEN. 41:1 2 YR.   **EPHRAIM** REPLACES LEVI IN THE INHERITANCE (GEN. 48:5; DEUT. 10:8,9).

BENJAMIN   Beginning about 1710 B.C. some Asiatics or Hebrews came to Egypt during the Hyksos period (page 66, of Ancient Egyptian History).   1765 B.C. AM 2290   110 YEARS (GEN. 50:22-26)   1606 B.C. AM 2369

MANASSEH REPLACES **JOSEPH** IN THE INHERITANCE (GEN. 48:5-22; JOSH. 14:4)

The tribe of Benjamin in Gen. 49:27, were warriors, who became the protectors of Judah. In Deut. 33:12 the beloved of the Lord (Judah) shall dwell in safety by him, and Judah shall dwell between Benjamin's shoulders. Among the Benjamite warriors to protect Judah were seven hundred chosen men able to throw left or right handed and not miss by an hair breadth (Judges 20: 15,16; 1 Chr. 12: 1-2). Saul, a Benjamite, son of Kish, stately, tall, and none like him among all the people, became the first King over all Israel (1 Sam. 9:10; see page 33). The chief of the fathers of Judah, Benjamin, and their portion of the Levites, returned from Babylonian captivity (Ezra 1:5). Descendants of these tribes, who still lived in the east after the Babylonian captivity, were the wise men who came seeking Jesus, when they saw the star (see pages 49, 53).

JACOB WAS 130 YEARS OLD WHEN HE WENT INTO EGYPT (GEN. 47:9).
THE 70 SOULS WHICH CAME INTO EGYPT (GEN. 46:7-27; DEUT. 10:22)

JACOB

LEAH (DIED IN CANAAN GEN. 49:31)   **ZILPAH**   **RACHEL** (DIED AT BETHLEHEM GEN. 35:16-20)   **BILHAH**

REUBEN AGE 46	SIMEON 45 YR.	LEVI 44 YR.	JUDAH 43 YR.	ISSACHAR 41 YR.	ZEBULON 40 YR.	DINAH 39 YR.	GAD 42 YR.	ASHER 41 YR.	JOSEPH 39 YR.	BENJAMIN 33 YR.	DAN 43 YR.	NAPHTALI 42 YR
HANOCH	JEMVEL	GERSHON	ER AND	TOLA	SERED	ZIPHION	JIMNAH		MANASSEH	BELAH	HUSHINI	JAHZEEL
PHALLY	JAMIN	KOHATH	ONAN	PHUVAH	ELON	HAGGI	ISHUAH		EPHRAIM	BECHER		GUNI
HEZRON	OHAD	MERARI	DIE IN	JOB	JAHLEEL	SHUNI	ISUI			ASHBEL		JEZER
CARMI	JACHIN		CANAAN	SHIMRON		EZBON	BERIAH		HEBER	GERA		SHILLEM
	ZOHAR		SHELAH			ERI	SERAH		MALCHIEL	NAAMAN		
	SHAUL		PHAREZ — HEZRON			ARODI	THEIR			EHI		
			ZERAH — HAMUL			ARELI	SISTER			ROSH		
										MUPPIM		
										HUPPIM		
										ARD		

GEN. 46:15	LEAH	35	When Jacob took his family down into Egypt, his youngest son, Benjamin, was 33 years old, and was the father of ten sons. At that time his father and brothers called him "the lad" (Gen. 43:8; Gen. 44:22-34), and "a little one" (Gen. 44:20). Isaac, when about to be sacrificed, was approximately 38 years old, and was called "the lad" (Gen. 22:12; see page 13).	JACOB HAD MANY DAUGHTERS ALSO (GEN. 37:35) (GEN. 46:7)
GEN. 46:18	ZILPAH	16		
GEN. 46:22	RACHEL	14		
GEN. 46:25	BILHAH	7		
GEN. 46:27		70		

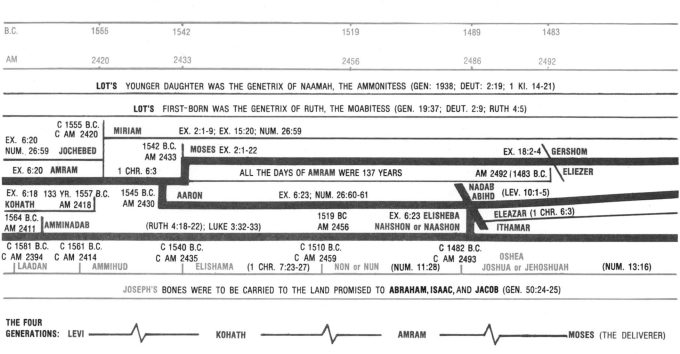

B.C.	1555	1542	1519	1489	1483
AM	2420	2433	2456	2486	2492

LOT'S YOUNGER DAUGHTER WAS THE GENETRIX OF NAAMAH, THE AMMONITESS (GEN: 1938; DEUT: 2:19; 1 KI. 14-21)

LOT'S FIRST-BORN WAS THE GENETRIX OF RUTH, THE MOABITESS (GEN. 19:37; DEUT. 2:9; RUTH 4:5)

C 1555 B.C.
C AM 2420 MIRIAM EX. 2:1-9; EX. 15:20; NUM. 26:59

EX. 6:20
NUM. 26:59 JOCHEBED 1542 B.C.
AM 2433 MOSES EX. 2:1-22 EX. 18:2-4 GERSHOM

EX. 6:20 AMRAM 1 CHR. 6:3 ALL THE DAYS OF AMRAM WERE 137 YEARS AM 2492 / 1483 B.C. ELIEZER

EX. 6:18 133 YR. 1557 B.C.
KOHATH AM 2418 1545 B.C.
AM 2430 AARON EX. 6:23; NUM. 26:60-61 NADAB
ABIHD (LEV. 10:1-5)

1564 B.C.
AM 2411 AMMINADAB (RUTH 4:18-22); LUKE 3:32-33) 1519 BC
AM 2456 EX. 6:23 ELISHEBA
NAHSHON or NAASHON ELEAZAR (1 CHR. 6:3)
ITHAMAR

C 1581 B.C. C 1561 B.C. C 1540 B.C. C 1510 B.C. C 1482 B.C.
C AM 2394 C AM 2414 C AM 2435 C AM 2459 C AM 2493 OSHEA
LAADAN AMMIHUD ELISHAMA (1 CHR. 7:23-27) NON or NUN (NUM. 11:28) JOSHUA or JEHOSHUAH (NUM. 13:16)

JOSEPH'S BONES WERE TO BE CARRIED TO THE LAND PROMISED TO ABRAHAM, ISAAC, AND JACOB (GEN. 50:24-25)

THE FOUR
GENERATIONS: LEVI ———⌇——— KOHATH ————⌇———— AMRAM ————⌇————MOSES (THE DELIVERER)

IN THE FOURTH GENERATION THEY (ISRAEL) SHALL COME HITHER AGAIN: . . . (GEN. 15:16) (SEE PAGE 21)

April 15, 1892 B.C., Abram entered Canaan. April 15, 1462 B.C., on the selfsame day, exactly 430 years later, the children of Israel departed from Rameses, Egypt (Num. 33:3). They sojourned half of that time in Canaan (215 years), and the other half of that time in Egypt (215 years). For their sojourning in Canaan, refer to Gen. 20:1; Gen. 21:34; Heb. 11:9. For their sojourning in Egypt, refer to Gen. 47:4; Deut. 26:5; Ps. 105:23; Acts 13:17. The children of Israel were serving in bitter and hard bondage, rigorously, when Moses was born (Ex. 1:13,14). And also that nation (Egypt), whom they shall serve, will I judge: and afterward shall they come out with great substance (Gen. 15:14; Acts 7:7). Now the sojourning of the children of Israel, who dwelt in Egypt, was four hundred and thirty years (Ex. 12:40). The clause "who dwelt in Egypt" specifies which children of Israel were spoken of, and does not suggest that they spent all of their sojourn in Egypt (see pages 18-21).

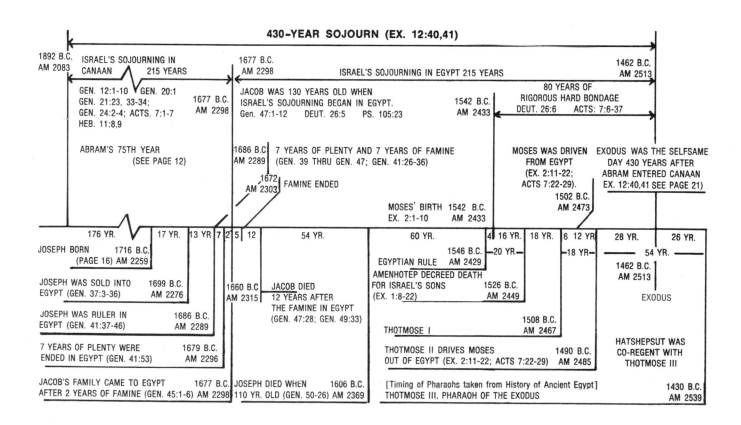

430-YEAR SOJOURN (EX. 12:40,41)

1892 B.C.
AM 2083 ISRAEL'S SOJOURNING IN CANAAN 215 YEARS 1677 B.C.
AM 2298 ISRAEL'S SOJOURNING IN EGYPT 215 YEARS 1462 B.C.
AM 2513

GEN. 12:1-10 GEN. 20:1
GEN. 21:23, 33-34;
GEN. 24:2-4; ACTS. 7:1-7;
HEB. 11:8,9 1677 B.C.
AM 2298 JACOB WAS 130 YEARS OLD WHEN ISRAEL'S SOJOURNING BEGAN IN EGYPT.
Gen. 47:1-12 DEUT. 26:5 PS. 105:23 1542 B.C.
AM 2433 80 YEARS OF RIGOROUS HARD BONDAGE
DEUT. 26:6 ACTS: 7:6-37

ABRAM'S 75TH YEAR
(SEE PAGE 12) 1686 B.C.
AM 2289 7 YEARS OF PLENTY AND 7 YEARS OF FAMINE
(GEN. 39 THRU GEN. 47; GEN. 41:26-36) MOSES WAS DRIVEN FROM EGYPT
(EX. 2:11-22;
ACTS 7:22-29) EXODUS WAS THE SELFSAME DAY 430 YEARS AFTER ABRAM ENTERED CANAAN
EX. 12:40,41 SEE PAGE 21)

1672
AM 2303 FAMINE ENDED 1502 B.C.
AM 2473

MOSES' BIRTH 1542 B.C.
EX. 2:1-10 AM 2433

176 YR.	17 YR.	13 YR	7	2	5	12	54 YR.	60 YR.	4	16 YR.	18 YR.	6	12 YR	28 YR.	26 YR.

JOSEPH BORN 1716 B.C.
(PAGE 16) AM 2259 1546 B.C.
AM 2429 20 YR— —18 YR— 54 YR. —
1462 B.C.
AM 2513

EGYPTIAN RULE

JOSEPH WAS SOLD INTO EGYPT (GEN. 37:3-36) 1699 B.C.
AM 2276 AMENHOTEP DECREED DEATH FOR ISRAEL'S SONS
(EX. 1:8-22) 1526 B.C.
AM 2449 EXODUS

1660 BC
AM 2315 JACOB DIED 12 YEARS AFTER THE FAMINE IN EGYPT
(GEN. 47:28; GEN. 49:33)

JOSEPH WAS RULER IN EGYPT (GEN. 41:37-46) 1686 B.C.
AM 2289 THOTMOSE I 1508 B.C.
AM 2467

7 YEARS OF PLENTY WERE ENDED IN EGYPT (GEN. 41:53) 1679 B.C.
AM 2296 HATSHEPSUT WAS CO-REGENT WITH THOTMOSE III

THOTMOSE II DRIVES MOSES OUT OF EGYPT (EX. 2:11-22; ACTS 7:22-29) 1490 B.C.
AM 2485

JACOB'S FAMILY CAME TO EGYPT AFTER 2 YEARS OF FAMINE (GEN. 45:1-6) 1677 B.C.
AM 2298 JOSEPH DIED WHEN 110 YR. OLD (GEN. 50-26) 1606 B.C.
AM 2369 [Timing of Pharaohs taken from History of Ancient Egypt]
THOTMOSE III, PHARAOH OF THE EXODUS 1430 B.C.
AM 2539

B.C.	1463		1462
	12th MO. MARCH 6th	←——— 40 DAYS OF PLAGUES IN EGYPT ———→	1st MO., 14th, OF APRIL
AM	2512		2513

LOT'S YOUNGER DAUGHTER WAS THE GENETRIX OF NAAMAH, A MOTHER IN JUDAH'S LINEAGE (GEN. 19:38; DEUT. 2:19; 1 KI. 14:21).

LOT'S FIRST-BORN WAS THE GENETRIX OF RUTH, THE GREAT-GRANDMOTHER OF KING DAVID (GEN. 19:37; RUTH 5:18-22).

MIRIAM   MIRIAM'S DAYS WERE TO THE FORTIETH YEAR OF ISRAEL'S WANDERINGS (NUM. 20:11).

MOSES   ALL THE DAYS OF MOSES THE DELIVERER WERE 120 YEARS (DEUT. 34:7-8).

AARON   ALL THE DAYS OF AARON WERE 123 YEARS (NUM. 20:28; NUM. 33:38-39).

ELEAZAR   ELEAZAR BECAME CHIEF OVER THE CHIEF LEVITES (NUM. 3:32; NUM. 4:16).

NAASHON   IN THE LINEAGE OF JUDAH TO CHRIST (RUTH 4:18-22; GEN. 49:8-10; MATT. 1:3-6; LUKE 3:32-33).

JOSHUA   JOSHUA WAS THE MINISTER (SERVANT) TO MOSES (EX. 24:13; EX. 33:11; NUM. 11:28).

JOSEPH   MOSES TOOK THE BONES OF JOSEPH WITH HIM (GEN. 50:25; EX. 13:19).

EGYPT 1463 B.C.		March 6th. March is Adar the 12th month. Moses was now 80 years old	Ex. 7: 7
EGYPT	Mar.	7 The miracle of Moses' rod, changing into a serpent	Ex. 7: 8-14
EGYPT	Mar. 8	The water in the rivers shall be turned into blood. In vessels of wood, and vessels of stone.	
	15	The seven days were fulfilled	Ex. 7:15-25
EGYPT	Mar.	16 The plague of the frogs upon all the land of Egypt	Ex. 8: 1- 7
EGYPT	Mar.	17 Pharaoh pleads for the frogs to be removed to-morrow	Ex. 8: 8-11
EGYPT	Mar.	18 The frogs die, and they were gathered together upon heaps	Ex. 8:12-15
EGYPT	Mar.	19 The dust of Egypt became lice. *Duplication impossible by the magicians*	Ex. 8:16-19
EGYPT	Mar.	20 Moses stands before Pharaoh, and promises the plague of flies to-morrow	Ex. 8:20-23
EGYPT	Mar.	21 The flies appear in Egypt, but Goshen was spared	Ex. 8:24-28
EGYPT	Mar.	22 The flies were removed	Ex. 8:29-32
EGYPT	Mar.	23 Moses warns Pharaoh of murrain on your cattle, which is in the field only	Ex. 9: 1- 5
EGYPT	Mar.	24 Only the cattle found in the fields of Egypt died, but none of Israel's	Ex. 9: 6
EGYPT	Mar.	25 Pharaoh finds that none of the Israelites cattle died	Ex. 9: 7
EGYPT	Mar.	26 Moses sprinkled ashes before Pharaoh causing boils and blains	Ex. 9: 8-12
EGYPT	Mar.	27 Grievous hail was to fall upon every man, and beast found in the field	Ex. 9:13-21
EGYPT	Mar.	28 Pharaoh's God-fearing servants are spared death by hail mixed with fire	Ex. 9:20-26
EGYPT	Mar.	29 At Moses' sign God stops the hail mingled with fire sparing the newly planted wheat, and rye crops	Ex. 9:27-35
EGYPT	Mar.	30 Pharaoh's life was raised up, to shew in him God's power for all the earth to know (Ex. 9:15-16). The locusts were foretold for to-morrow	Ex.10: 1- 6
EGYPT	Mar.	31 Pharaoh again refused to let the women, and children, and flocks go. The east wind was upon the land all that day, and all that night	Ex.10: 7-13
EGYPT 1462 B.C.		April is Abib, the first month of the year to you (Ex. 12:2; Ex. 13:4)	Ex.12: 1- 2
EGYPT	Apr.	1 In the morning the east wind brought the locusts	Ex.10:14-15
EGYPT	Apr.	2 A mighty strong west wind carried the locusts into the Red Sea	Ex.10:16-20
EGYPT	Apr. 3	Three days of thick darkness that could be felt in all Egypt, but the children of Israel had	
	5	light in their dwellings	Ex.10:21-23
EGYPT	Apr.	6 Pharaoh will not see Moses again. Moses leaves in great anger (Ex. 11:8-10)	Ex.10:24-29
EGYPT	Apr.	7 God promises one more plague upon Egypt. The firstborn of Pharaoh, unto the firstborn of the maidservant, and the cattle shall die	Ex.11: 1- 7
EGYPT	Apr.	8 God commands Moses regarding the beginning of months (Ex. 13:4), and the taking of the passover lamb, readying for the passover celebration	Ex.12: 1-20
EGYPT	Apr.	9 Moses delivered God's commands to Israel. One law shall be to the home-born, and the stranger sojourning among you. Israel did God's command	Ex.12:22-28
EGYPT	Apr.	10 The tenth day every man took a lamb according to his house	Ex.12: 3- 6
EGYPT	Apr.	11-13 Moses' fame in Egypt enabled Israel to strip Egypt of her wealth	Ex.12:33-36
RAMESES	Apr.	14 Israel took the lamb according to their families, and killed the passover. The passover was eaten. The blood was applied to the door. At midnight Egypt's firstborn died (Ex. 12:29). Pharaoh orders the Israelites to leave shortly after midnight (Ex. 12:30-32).	
THURSDAY NIGHT			
14		*Egypt's 40 days of plagues were ended*	EX.12:40-42
RAMESES	Apr.	15 The 430 years of Israel's sojourning were completed at Rameses (Num. 33:3-8; Page 21).	

| B.C. | 1462 | Israel triumphed over death on Sunday April 17th, 1462 B.C. (Ex. 14:29-30). | 1462 |
| AM | 2513 | This was the type of Christ's triumph over death, the selfsame day, A.D. 29 (see page 59, 62). | 2513 |

LOT YOUNGER		LOT'S
LOT FIRSTBORN		LOT'S
MIRIAM		MIRIAM
MOSES		MOSES
AARON		AARON
ELEAZAR		ELEAZAR
NAASHON		NAASHON
JOSHUA		JOSHUA
JOSEPH'S BONES		JOSEPH'S BONES

1462 B.C. RAMESES to SUCCOTH	Apr. 15,	On the morrow after the passover, Israel went out with an high hand in the sight of all the Egyptians ("Selfsame Day" Ex. 12:41; page 62) ....Num. 33:3-8
	Apr. 15,	About 600,000 footmen, beside children, and the mixed multitude, and flocks, and very much cattle. Unleavened bread was baked first at Succoth ....Ex. 12:37-39
		One law shall be to the homeborn, and the stranger sojourning among you ....Ex. 12:43-51
to		Remember this day in the month Abib, and keep the passover a memorial from year to year. Moses took the bones of Joseph with him ....Ex. 13: 1-19
ETHAM to	Apr. 16,	God gave Israel the cloud to lead by day, and the pillar of fire to give them light by night. God's protection in all their journeyings ....Ex. 13:21-22
PIHAHIROTH that evening and	Apr. 16,	Israel encamps between Migdol, and the sea, before Baal-Zephon mountains ....Ex. 14: 1- 4
		Pharaoh overtook Israel beside Pihahiroth by the sea, before Baal-Zephon mountains, and was separated from Israel by the Angel of God in a cloud, which was darkness to the Egyptians, but light by night to Israel ....Ex. 14: 5-20
VERY EARLY in the morning	Apr. 17,	Israel passed through the Red Sea on dry ground. The Egyptians pursued into the midst of the sea ("depths" in Ex. 15:5). Not one of the Egyptians remained alive when the morning appeared (Neh. 9:11) ....Ex. 14:21-31

22

THE TEN COMMANDMENTS WERE GIVEN AUDIBLY FOR ALL ISRAEL TO HEAR IN JUNE 1462 B.C.

B.C.	1462	1462	1462
	FROM RAMESES APRIL 15TH	EXODUS APRIL 17TH	2 MONTHS OF JOURNEYING TO JUNE 15TH AT SINAI
AM	2513	2513	2513

LOT'S YOUNGER DAUGHTER (GEN. 19:38; 1 KI. 14:21)

LOT'S FIRSTBORN (GEN. 19:37; DEUT. 2:9; RUTH 4:5, 18-22)

MIRIAM DIED IN 1423 B.C. (NUM. 20:1)

ALL THE DAYS OF MOSES ARE 120 YR. (DEUT. 34:7-8)

ALL THE DAYS OF AARON WERE 123 YR. (NUM. 20:28; 33:38-39)

ELEAZAR, CHIEF OF THE LEVITES (NUM. 3:32; 4:16; JOSH. 24:33)

NAASHON (RUTH 4:18-22; MATT. 1:3-6; LUKE 3:32-33)

JOSHUA EX. 24:13; EX. 33:11; NUM. 11:28

JOSEPH (GEN. 50:25; EX. 13:19).

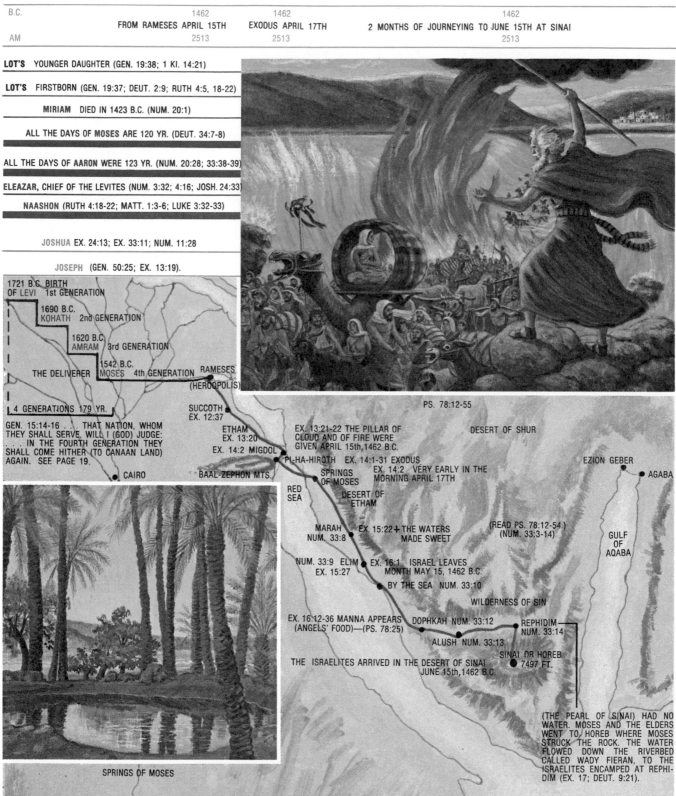

1721 B.C. BIRTH OF LEVI 1st GENERATION

1690 B.C. KOHATH 2nd GENERATION

1620 B.C. AMRAM 3rd GENERATION

1542 B.C. THE DELIVERER MOSES 4th GENERATION RAMESES (HEROOPOLIS)

4 GENERATIONS 179 YR.

GEN. 15:14-16 . . . THAT NATION, WHOM THEY SHALL SERVE, WILL I (GOD) JUDGE: . . . IN THE FOURTH GENERATION THEY SHALL COME HITHER (TO CANAAN LAND) AGAIN. SEE PAGE 19.

CAIRO

SUCCOTH EX. 12:37

ETHAM EX. 13:20

EX. 14:2 MIGDOL

PI-HA-HIROTH EX. 14:1-31 EXODUS

BAAL-ZEPHON MTS.

SPRINGS OF MOSES

EX. 14:2 VERY EARLY IN THE MORNING APRIL 17TH

RED SEA

DESERT OF ETHAM

PS. 78:12-55

EX. 13:21-22 THE PILLAR OF CLOUD AND OF FIRE WERE GIVEN APRIL 15th, 1462 B.C.

DESERT OF SHUR

EZION GEBER

AGABA

GULF OF AQABA

MARAH NUM. 33:8

EX. 15:22 + THE WATERS MADE SWEET

(READ PS. 78:12-54.) (NUM. 33:3-14)

NUM. 33:9 ELIM EX. 15:27

EX. 16:1 ISRAEL LEAVES MONTH MAY 15, 1462 B.C.

BY THE SEA NUM. 33:10

WILDERNESS OF SIN

EX. 16:12-36 MANNA APPEARS (ANGELS' FOOD)—(PS. 78:25)

DOPHKAH NUM. 33:12

ALUSH NUM. 33:13

REPHIDIM NUM. 33:14

THE ISRAELITES ARRIVED IN THE DESERT OF SINAI JUNE 15th, 1462 B.C.

SINAI OR HOREB 7497 FT.

(THE PEARL OF SINAI) HAD NO WATER. MOSES AND THE ELDERS WENT TO HOREB WHERE MOSES STRUCK THE ROCK. THE WATER FLOWED DOWN THE RIVERBED CALLED WADY FIERAN, TO THE ISRAELITES ENCAMPED AT REPHIDIM (EX. 17; DEUT. 9:21).

SPRINGS OF MOSES

1462 B.C. In the month of June, THE TEN COMMANDMENTS were given audibly to all the people to hear (Deut. 4:10-15; 5:22-27; 9:10). Israel feared, wanting Moses and not God to speak to them, Ex. 20:1-21.

1462 B.C. In the third month Sivan (June), after the 15th day, Jethro Moses' father-in-law, and Moses' family met Moses at Mt. Sinai (Ex. 18:1-12). Jethro was also known as the priest of Midian in Ex. 2:16; Reuel in Ex. 2:18; Jethro in Ex. 3:1; Raguel the Midianite in Num. 10:29; and the Kenite in Judges 1:16.

For the deliverance of the Israelites and Moses, from the Egyptians, Jethro blessed the Lord. Jethro offered a burnt offering and sacrifices to God. Aaron came, and all the elders of Israel, to eat bread with Moses' father-in-law before God (Ex. 18:10-12).

Moses accepted Jethro's wise counsel, to appoint judges over thousands, hundreds, fifties, and tens, leaving the very great matters for Moses to judge, established Moses as the first judge over all Israel in the month of June, 1462 B.C. (see page 14) Ex. 18:13-27.

B.C.	1462		1462
AM	2513	AT SINAI	2513

LOT'S YOUNGER DAUGHTER THE GENETRIX OF NAAMAH, A MOTHER IN CHRIST'S LINEAGE (GEN. 19:38; DEUT. 2:19; 1 KI. 14:21)

LOT'S FIRSTBORN THE GENETRIX OF RUTH, A MOTHER IN CHRIST'S LINEAGE (GEN. 19:37; DEUT. 2:9; LUKE 3:32)

MIRIAM DIED IN THE FIRST MONTH OF THE FORTIETH YEAR (NUM. 20:1)

ALL THE DAYS OF MOSES WERE 120 YR. (DEUT. 34:7,8)

AARON (Ps. 106:16)	The calendar year records the day of the week on which April 14 falls, which is passover day.	(Num. 20:28; 33:38-39)
ELEAZAR	The date is always the same but the day of the week varies.	(Num. 3:32; 4:16; Josh. 24:33)
NAASHON (Ruth 4:18-22)	Pentecost Sunday is always the same day of the week, but the date varies from June 3 thru 9. Pentecost Sundays are circled in red on (page 64).	(Matt. 1:3-6; Luke 3:32-33)

April (Abib or Nisan) Israel's first month of the year (Ex. 12:2; 13:4; 23:15; 34:18; Neh. 2:1; Esther 3:7). *1st day* of every month is called beginnings of months or new moons, a day of feasting, blowing of trumpets for a memorial before your God (Num. 10:10; 28:11-14; Ps. 81:3). *10th day,* the passover lamb is chosen (Ex. 12:3-5). *14th day,* the passover is eaten in the evening. (Ex. 12:6-14; Lev. 23:5; Num. 9:2-5; 28:16; Ezek. 45:21). *15th to 21st* was the feast of the passover. The first and last days of the feast, the 15th and 21st, were sabbath days, holy convocations, when no manner of work was to be done. All males 20 years old and upward must appear with a gift (Ex. 12:15-20; 23:14-17; Lev. 23:6-8; Num. 28:17-25; 2 Chr. 35:1). *21st* is a solemn assembly (Deut. 16:1-8, 16-17). [The 29th jubilee year, A.D. 29, Jesus died (page 57,62). He is our passover (1 Cor. 5:7), slain to set us free from sin (Matt. 27:15; Mk. 15:6; Luke 23:17; John 18:39).]	May (Zif or Ziv) 2nd mo. (1 Ki. 6:1). *1st day* of the month, new moon celebration. *14th,* the second passover is kept by those defiled by a dead body, or on a journey, when the first passover was kept (Num. 9:6-14).	June (Sivan) 3rd mo. (Esther 8:9). *1st day* of the month, new moon celebration. Pentecost Sunday falls during June 3 thru 9, fifty days after passover sabbath (a Saturday), (Lev. 23:10-21; Deut. 16:9-10). It is also called the feast of harvest (Ex. 23:16), and the feast of weeks, of the firstfruits of wheat harvest (Ex. 34:22; Deut. 16:10). Each male must bring a gift (Deut. 16:16-17). Pentecost Sundays are circled in red (page 64).
July (Tammuz in the Jewish calendar is the 4th month). *1st day* of the month, new moon celebration.	August (Ab Jewish cal.) the 5th mo. (Ezra 7:8-9). *1st day* of the month, new moon celebration.	September (Elul) 6th mo. (Neh. 6:15). *1st day* of the month, new moon celebration.
October (Tishri in the Jewish calendar) 7th mo. (Ethanim, 1 Ki. 8:2). *1st day,* new moon celebration. Of the twelve new moons, October 1st is the only holy convocation feast (Lev. 23:24; Num. 29:1; Ps. 81:3). *10th day,* the day of atonement, a day of afflicting the soul (fasting) (Lev. 16:29; Lev. 23:27,29,32). Every seventh year the law must be read before all Israel (Deut. 31:9-13; Jer. 36:6). *10th day,* every 49th year the trumpet of the jubilee is sounded (Lev. 25:9; Lev. 25; 8-55). All prisoners set free (Jer. 34:9). *15th* to the *21st* the feast of tabernacles or feast of ingathering. They shall dwell in booths seven days (Ex. 23:14-17; Lev. 23:34-44; Deut. 16:13-17; Neh. 8:14). All males 20 years old and upward must appear with a gift (Ex. 23:14-17; Deut. 16:16-17). *15th to 21st,* the feast of tabernacles, special offerings are made each day, an holy convocation (Lev. 23:36-39; Num. 29:12-39; Ezek. 45:25). *22nd day,* the 8th day, is a solemn assembly (Num. 29:35).	November (Bul) 8th mo. (1 Ki. 6:38). *1st day* of the month, new moon celebration. God's 12-month calendar (1 Ki. 4:7 Rev. 22:2).	December (Chisleu) 9th mo. (Neh. 1:1; Zech. 7:1) *1st day* of the month, new moon celebration. In the winterhouse the ninth month (Jer. 36:22). At Jerusalem was the feast of dedication. It was winter (John 10:22).
January (Tebeth) (10th month, Esther 2:16). *1st day* of the month, new moon celebration.	February (Sebat) 11th month (Zech. 1:7). *1st day* of the month, new moon celebration.	March (Adar), the 12th Mo. (Esther 3:7; 13:8,12). *1st day* of the month, new moon celebration. *14th* and *15th* purim feast is by decree of Queen Esther in 473 B.C. (Esther 9:17-32).

B.C.	1462
	AT SINAI
AM	2513

LOT'S YOUNGER DAUGHTER (DEUT. 2:19; GEN. 19:38).

LOT'S FIRSTBORN (GEN. 19:37; RUTH 4:18-22).

MIRIAM DIED IN 1423 B.C.   NUM. 20:1

MOSES THE DELIVERER 120 YR.   DEUT. 34:7-8

AARON DIED ON THE 1st DAY OF THE 5th MO. 1423 B.C.

ELEAZAR   NUM. 3:32; 4:16 JOSH. 24:33; 1 CHR. 6:1-15

NAASHON IN JUDAH'S LINEAGE (GEN. 49:8-10).

DEUT. 31:23   JOSHUA

JOSEPH

Holiness to the Lord
(EX. 28:36-38; 39:30).

Aaron died on his birthday
August 1st, 1423 B.C.   (page 28)

A mitre for Aaron the high priest and
bonnets for his sons (EX. 28:36-40;
EX. 29:6-9; EX. 39:30; LEV. 8:9)

Engraved Onyx shoulder stones (EX. 28:9-13).

The breastplate (Ex. 39:8-21) was made double like a pocket, and **THE URIM AND THUMMIM** was put into the breastplate of judgment, which was worn upon the High Priest's heart (Ex. 28:30; Lev. 8:8). God gave these judgments to Moses (Ex. 21:1). Moses wrote all the words of the Lord, and all the judgments in a book called **THE BOOK OF THE COVENANT** (Ex. 24:3-8). They were based upon **THE TEN COMMANDMENTS,** written with the finger of God, on tables of stone, and carried in **THE ARK OF THE COVENANT.** All Israel promised to obey God's judgments. When they obeyed, they were blest, when they disobeyed, they were cursed. Thus, **URIM AND THUMMIM,** brought the blessing or cursing, as God commanded (Duet. 11:26-28), life and good, or death and evil (Deut. 30:15), depending upon their obedience or disobedience. This covenant became binding when Moses sprinkled both it, and the people with blood (Ex. 24:8). The New Testament (covenant) came into force when Jesus shed his blood (Lev. 17:11; Matt. 26:28; Heb. 9:15-28; 10:1-22). The High Priest needed only to refer to the book of the covenant in his breastplate to find God's written judgments.

Among the laws and judgments, written were: the laws to live by, meats that could be eaten, the blueprint for the tabernacle, garments and services for the priests, the death penalty, establishing the times for the yearly Passover, and the Day of Atonement, also the celebration of sabbatical and jubilee years (Lev. 25). A judge must ask council of **URIM AND THUMMIM** (Num. 27:21). A king was to copy this book of the law, and read therein all the days of his life (Ex. 24:3-8; Deut. 17:18-19; 31:9-13; Josh. 1:8); Read Ex. 20 through 40; Lev. 1-27 ; see page 31 .

The golden censer
(LEV. 10:1; LEV. 16:12).

During the last month of Moses' life, he re-wrote the law, in Deuteronomy , which was to be kept in the side of **THE ARK OF THE COVENANT.** This book was a repetition of the original covenant, with needful additions for the success of Israel, when they came into the promised land (Deut. 31:9; 24-26).

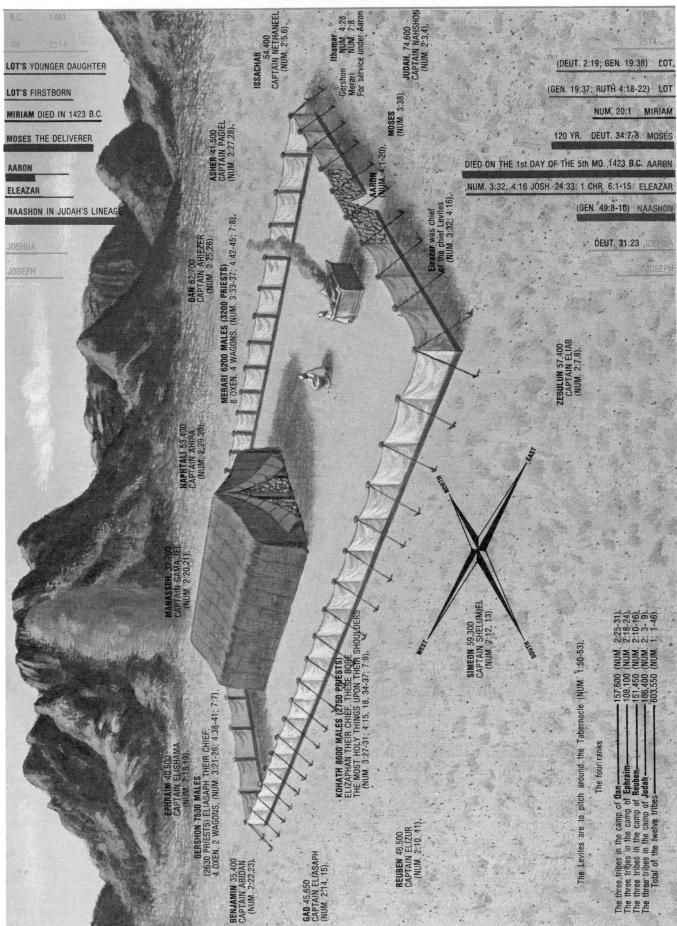

B.C. 1461

AM 2514

LOT'S YOUNGER DAUGHTER

LOT'S FIRSTBORN

MIRIAM DIED IN 1423 B.C.

MOSES THE DELIVERER

AARON

ELEAZAR

NAASHON IN JUDAH'S LINEAGE

JOSHUA

JOSEPH

1461

2514

(DEUT. 2:19; GEN. 19:38) LOT

(GEN. 19:37; RUTH 4:18-22) LOT

NUM. 20:1 MIRIAM

120 YR. DEUT. 34:7-8 MOSES

DIED ON THE 1st DAY OF THE 5th MO. 1423 B.C. AARON

NUM. 3:32; 4:16 JOSH. 24:33; 1 CHR. 6:1-15 ELEAZAR

(GEN. 49:8-10) NAASHON

DEUT. 31:23 JOSHUA

JOSEPH

ISSACHAR 54,400 CAPTAIN NETHANEEL (NUM. 2:5,6).

Ithamar NUM. 4:28
Gershon NUM. 7:8
Merari
For service under Aaron

JUDAH, 74,600 CAPTAIN NAHSHON (NUM. 2:3,4).

MOSES (NUM. 3:38).

AARON (NUM. 4:1-20).

Eleazar was chief of the chief Levites (NUM. 3:32; 4:16).

ASHER 41,500 CAPTAIN PAGIEL (NUM. 2:27,28).

DAN 62,700 CAPTAIN AHIEZER (NUM. 2:25,26).

MERARI 6200 MALES (3200 PRIESTS) 8 OXEN, 4 WAGONS. (NUM. 3:33-37; 4:42-45; 7:8).

ZEBULUN 57,400 CAPTAIN ELIAB (NUM. 2:7,8).

NAPHTALI 53,400 CAPTAIN AHIRA (NUM. 2:29,30).

MANASSEH 32,200 CAPTAIN GAMALIEL (NUM. 2:20,21).

EAST

NORTH

WEST

SOUTH

KOHATH 8600 MALES (2750 PRIESTS) ELIZAPHAN THEIR CHIEF. THESE BORE THE MOST HOLY THINGS UPON THEIR SHOULDERS (NUM. 3:27-31; 4:15, 18, 34-37; 7:9).

SIMEON 59,300 CAPTAIN SHELUMIEL (NUM. 2:12, 13).

EPHRAIM 40,500 CAPTAIN ELISHAMA (NUM. 2:18,19).

GERSHON 7500 MALES (2630 PRIESTS) ELIASAPH THEIR CHIEF 4 OXEN, 2 WAGONS. (NUM. 3:21-26; NUM. 4:38-41; 7:7).

BENJAMIN 35,400 CAPTAIN ABIDAN (NUM. 2:22,23).

GAD 45,650 CAPTAIN ELIASAPH (NUM. 2:14, 15).

REUBEN 46,500 CAPTAIN ELIZUR (NUM. 2:10, 11).

The Levites are to pitch around the Tabernacle (NUM. 1:50-53).

The four ranks

The three tribes in the camp of Dan ———— 157,600 (NUM. 2:25-31).
The three tribes in the camp of Ephraim —— 108,100 (NUM. 2:18-24).
The three tribes in the camp of Reuben —— 151,450 (NUM. 2:10-16).
The three tribes in the camp of Judah —— 186,400 (NUM. 2: 3 - 9).
Total of the twelve tribes ———————— 603,550 (NUM. 1: 1-46).

B.C.	1461		1461
AM	2514	April 8th,1461 B.C., right after the consecration of Aaron and his four sons, Nadab and Abihu offered strange fire and were slain of God (Lev. 8:12, 23-24; Lev. 9:1; Lev. 10:1-11)	2514

MIRIAM		MIRIAM
MOSES		MOSES
AARON		AARON
ELEAZAR		ELEAZAR
NAASHON		NAASHON
JOSHUA		JOSHUA
JOSEPH'S BONES		JOSEPH'S BONES

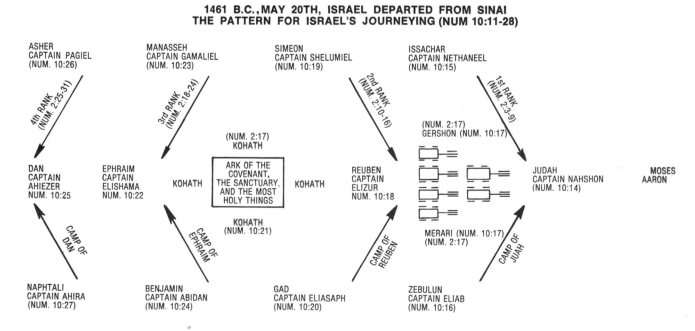

Nadab and Abihu offered strange fire and were slain of God (Lev. 10:1-11)

1461 B.C., MAY 20TH, ISRAEL DEPARTED FROM SINAI
THE PATTERN FOR ISRAEL'S JOURNEYING (NUM 10:11-28)

ASHER CAPTAIN PAGIEL (NUM. 10:26)

MANASSEH CAPTAIN GAMALIEL (NUM. 10:23)

SIMEON CAPTAIN SHELUMIEL (NUM. 10:19)

ISSACHAR CAPTAIN NETHANEEL (NUM. 10:15)

4th RANK (NUM. 2:25-31)

3rd RANK (NUM. 2:18-24)

2nd RANK (NUM. 2:10-16)

1st RANK (NUM. 2:3-9)

(NUM. 2:17) KOHATH

(NUM. 2:17) GERSHON (NUM. 10:17)

DAN CAPTAIN AHIEZER NUM. 10:25

EPHRAIM CAPTAIN ELISHAMA NUM. 10:22

KOHATH

ARK OF THE COVENANT, THE SANCTUARY, AND THE MOST HOLY THINGS

KOHATH

REUBEN CAPTAIN ELIZUR NUM. 10:18

JUDAH CAPTAIN NAHSHON (NUM. 10:14)

MOSES AARON

KOHATH (NUM. 10:21)

MERARI (NUM. 10:17) (NUM. 2:17)

CAMP OF DAN

CAMP OF EPHRAIM

CAMP OF REUBEN

CAMP OF JUAH

NAPHTALI CAPTAIN AHIRA (NUM. 10:27)

BENJAMIN CAPTAIN ABIDAN (NUM. 10:24)

GAD CAPTAIN ELIASAPH (NUM. 10:20)

ZEBULUN CAPTAIN ELIAB (NUM. 10:16)

B.C.		1461	1461
AM		2514	2514

LOT TO NAAMAH
(GEN. 19:38; DEUT. 2:19; 1 KI. 14:21)

LOT TO RUTH
(GEN. 19:37; DEUT. 2:9; RUTH 4:5, 18-22)

MIRIAM   NUM. 20:1

MOSES   120 YEARS   (DEUT. 34:7-8)

AARON 123 YR. (NUM. 20:26-29; 33:38-39)

ELEAZAR THE CHIEF LEVITE
(NUM. 34:17; JOSH. 14:1)

SALMON
(GEN. 49:8-10; MATT. 1:3-6; LUKE 3:32-33)

JOSHUA, SERVANT OF MOSES
(NUM. 27:18-22; DEUT. 31:23)

JOSEPH BURIED IN CANAAN
(GEN. 50:24-25; EX. 13:19; JOSH. 24:32)

1461 B.C. May 20th the second month, Israel left Sinai. (See travel pattern page 26.) Moses invites Hobab his brother-in-law, who knew the country, to go with them. His reward would be to later share God's goodness to Israel (Num. 10:11-36).

May 23rd, After three days' journey, at Taberah, because Israel complained, God's fire consumed them in the utmost part of the camp (Num. 10:33-36; 11:1-3).

Thirty days of quails were given at Kibrothhattaavah, where the Lord smote the people with a very great plague (Num. 11:4-35; Deut. 9:22).

At Hazeroth Miriam was smitten with leprosy because she and Aaron spake against Moses. Miriam was shut out from the camp for seven days. (Num. 12:1-16).

THE ELEVEN-DAY JOURNEY FROM SINAI TO KADESH-BARNEA (DEUT. 1:2), REQUIRED APPROXIMATELY NINETY DAYS BECAUSE OF ISRAEL'S COMPLAINING AND LUSTING.

Approximately August 20th, from Kadesh-Barnea in the wilderness of Paran (Zin) (Num. 13:3,26; 27:14; Deut. 32:51), twelve rulers were sent to spy out the land of Canaan. After forty days, about September 30th, two spies returned with one cluster of giant-sized grapes, showing the abundance of the land. All Canaan was inhabited by giants, living in great walled cities. Of the twelve spies only Caleb of Judah's tribe, and Joshua (Oshea) of Ephraim were ready to possess Canaan, saying they were well able to overcome the giants. (Num. 13:1-33).

ENMISHPAT GEN.14:7
KADESH-BARNEA

MERIBAH

PARAN   OR ZIN

RAMESES
EX. 12:37

SUCCOTH   BITTER
EX. 12:37; 13:20   LAKES

ETHAM
EX. 13:20

EX. 14:2 MIGDOL

EGYPT   BAAL-ZEPHON MTS.   PI-HA-HIROTH
EX. 14:2

SPRINGS
OF MOSES

RED

EZION GEBER

ELATH   AGABA

MARAH
NUM. 33:8

HAZEROTH
NUM. 11:35; 33:17

ELIM
NUM. 33:9

1460 B.C. ISRAEL COULD HAVE ENTERED CANAAN, BUT BECAUSE OF THE EVIL REPORT, ISRAEL WAS SENTENCED TO A TOTAL OF FORTY YEARS OF WANDERING. TWO YEARS FROM EGYPT TO DEPARTURE FROM KADESH-BARNEA, AND THIRTY-EIGHT YEARS YET, BEFORE THEY ENTERED CANAAN (Deut. 2:14; Num. 14:33-35).

BY THE SEA
NUM. 33:10

SEA

KIBROTH HATTAAVAH
NUM. 11:34
NUM. 33:16

DOPHKAH
NUM. 33:12

REPHIDIM
NUM. 33:14

TABERAH
NUM. 11:18

ALUSH
NUM. 33:13

1461 B.C. At Sinai in April, the first month, on the first day of the month, the TABERNACLE was first reared up (Ex. 40:2, 17-19; Num. 9:15-23; page 49).

MT. SINAI
(HOREB)
7497 FT.

See pattern of encampment on page 25.   See pattern of journeying on page 26.

1461 B.C. In October, Moses, because of God's anger with him, will not go into Canaan. (Num. 20:12; 27:12-14; Deut. 1:37).

THIRTY-EIGHT YEARS LATER (see page 28)

1423 B.C. Moses, because of unbelief at Meribah was denied entrance to Canaan. (Num. 20:1-13; 27:14; Deut. 3:25-27).

MIRIAM, AARON, AND MOSES DIE IN 1423 B.C.
ISRAEL'S 40 YEARS OF WANDERING COMPLETED APRIL 10, 1422 B.C.

B.C.	1461		1423	1422
AT KADESH-BARNEA		THE BEGINNING OF SABBATICAL AND JUBILEE-YEAR TIMING (LEV. 25; DEUT. 31:9-13; PAGE 57).		
AM	2514		2552	2553

LOT TO NAAMAH   THE AMMONITESS, WIFE OF SOLOMON   (GEN. 19:37; DEUT. 2:9; RUTH 4). 19; 1 KI. 14:21).

LOT TO RUTH   THE MOABITES, WIFE OF BOAZ   (GEN. 19:37; DEUT. 2:9; RUTH 4).

ELEAZAR

MIRIAM   DIES AT KADESH-BARNEA IN THE FIRST MONTH, APRIL (NUM. 20:1).   1423 B.C. AM 2552

RUTH

MOSES   DIED ON MT. PISGAH ON THE 6th DAY OF THE 12th MONTH HIS 120th BIRTHDAY (DEUT. 31:1-2; 34:7).   1423 B.C. AM 2552

SALMON

AARON   DIED ON MT. HOR THE 1st DAY OF THE 5th MONTH, AUGUST (NUM. 20:25-29; 33:38-39).   1423 B.C. AM 2552

JOSHUA

ELEAZAR   SUCCEEDS AARON AS THE HIGH PRIEST (NUM. 20:26-29; 33:38-39).

SALMON   IN THE LINEAGE OF CHRIST (RUTH 4:18-22; MATT. 1:3-6; LUKE 3:32-33; GEN. 49:8-10).

JOSHUA   THE SUCCESSOR OF MOSES (NUM. 27:18-22; DEUT. 31:23).

JOSEPH'S   BONES WERE BURIED AT SCHECHEM (GEN. 50:24-25; JOSH. 24:32)   1422 B.C. AM 2553

Sinai to Moseroth (Num. 33:16-30) Mosera (Deut. 10:6) to Kadesh (Num. 13:3,26; 27:14).

1461 B.C., In October, at Kadesh-barnea, because of the evil report of the ten spies, Israel rebelled against God, for which all that were numbered from twenty years and upward, would die, and not see the promised land. Israel's total wanderings shall be forty years. Israel mourned greatly, yet went to war presumptuously against the Amalekites. They and the Canaanites smote Israel unto Hormah (Mt. Hor) (Num. 14:1-45; Deut. 1:41-45).

Korah, a Levite, Dathan and Abiram, and sons of Reuben, rebel against Moses. They and their families went down alive into the pit (Num. 16:1-40).

On the morrow, Israel murmured against Moses and Aaron, accusing them of killing the people of the Lord. 14,700 Israelites died before Aaron's atonement, ordered by Moses, stopped the plague of God on Israel (Num. 16:41-50).

Aaron's budding rod was proof to Israel of Aaron's priesthood (Num. 17:1-13; Heb. 9:4).

1461 B.C., Kadesh to Horhagidgad to Ezion-Gaber (Num. 14:25; 33:32-35).
c-1460 B.C., From Ezion-Gaber to Kadesh-Barnea (Num. 33:36).
After many days at Kadesh (Deut. 1:46) (Approximately 37 years).
1423 B.C., April, the 1st mo., Miriam died at Kadesh Barnea (Num. 20:1).
1423 B.C., August, (5th mo., 1st day) Aaron died on Mt. Hor (Num. 20:24-29; 33:37-39).

1423 B.C., Israel complained of the long way around, lack of bread, water, and being tired of manna, so God sent fiery serpents among them. The people were spared when they looked upon the brass serpent made by Moses. Israel called it Nehushtan, keeping it to Hezekiah's reign 724 B.C. (Num. 21:4-9; 2 Ki. 18:4; see page 4).

Feb. 1, 1423 B.C., The Eleventh month Moses spoke unto the children of Israel orally all God's commandments (Deut. 1:3).

Feb. 2nd Moses wrote all the words of the covenant made at Horeb, plus God's commandments, given in the plains **thru** of Moab (Deut. 29:1). This book of the law (Urim and Thummim) was God's **Mar. 5th,** covenant to govern Israel, and all mankind (Deut. 17:8-20; Deut. 7:9; Deut. 31:9-13).

Mar. 6, 1423 B.C., Moses died on his 120th birthday (Deut. 31:1; Deut. 34:7).

Apr. 5, 1422 B.C., Thirty days of mourning for Moses were ended (Deut. 34:8).

Apr. 6, 1422 B.C., Israel was to cross Jordan within three days (Josh. 1:11). Two spies were sent to Jericho. Rahab hid the spies, who promised to save all her family alive (Josh. 2:1-22).

Apr. 7, 1422 B.C., Joshua's spies hid in the mountains (Josh. 2:15-16). **thru Apr. 9,** Israel prepared to cross Jordan (Josh. 1:11; Josh. 3:2-4).

Apr. 9, 1422 B.C., Early, Joshua brought all Israel to Jordan (Josh. 3:1). Joshua's spies brought back a good report (Josh. 2:23-24) (Compare Neh. 9:24-26). Joshua assured Israel of God's wonders on the morrow (Josh. 3:5).

Apr. 10, 1422 B.C. The 1st mo., the 10th day, all Israel crossed Jordan (Josh. 4:19; Josh. 3:15; I Chr. 12:15).

EDREI NUM. 21:33

ZAN ZUMMIMS DEUT. 2:20

SHECHEM JOSH. 24:32

LAND OF THE AMORITES JUD. 10:8

AMMON

EMMIMS DEUT. 2:10-11

JERICHO   JOSH. 2:1; 3:1   ABEL SHITTIM

HESHBON NUM. 26:34

GILGAL   BETH PEOR   MT. NERO   MT. PISGAH

MOAB

ISRAEL'S WANDERINGS DEUT. 2:14; NUM. 14:33-38

EGYPT TO KADESH	2 YR.
KADESH TO CANAAN	38 YR.
TOTAL	40 YR.

ENMISHPAT GEN. 14:7 KADESH-BARNEA

WILDERNESS OF   NUM. 12:16 PARAN OR ZIN   NUM. 13:3-26   NUM. 27:14

MT. HOR DEUT. 32:5

EGYPT

RIVER OF

EZION-GEBER (ELATH)

AGABA

GULF

OF

AGABA

B.C.	1422		1422

The flooded Jordan stood up upon an heap (Joshua 3:15-16).

AM	2553		2553

LOT TO **NAAMAH**   THE AMMONITESS WIFE OF **SOLOMON**   (GEN. 19:38; DEUT. 2:19; 1 KI. 14:21).

ELEAZAR AND **JOSHUA** LEAD ISRAEL (NUM. 34:17; JOSH. 14:1-2; JOSH. 19:51) **ELEAZAR'S** LINEAGE (1 CHR. 6:1-15).

LOT TO **RUTH** THE MOABITESS WIFE OF **BOAZ** (GEN. 19:37; DEUT. 2:9; RUTH 4:10).

SALMON   IN THE LINEAGE OF CHRIST (RUTH 4:18-22; MATT. 1:3-6; LUKE 3:32-33).

JOSHUA   OF THE SEED OF JOSEPH SUCCEEDS **MOSES** (NUM. 13:8; DEUT. 34:9; JOSH. 1:1-9; 1 CHR. 7:22-27).

April 10, 1422 B.C., All males were circumcised at Gilgal near Jericho (Josh. 5:2-9).
April 14, 1422 B.C., Israel's first passover in Canaan (Josh. 5:10).
April 15, 1422 B.C., Israel ate of the old corn of Canaan (Josh. 5:11).
April 16, 1422 B.C., The manna ceased (Josh. 5:12; see page 62).

JOSHUA LEADS ISRAEL THROUGH THE JORDAN.

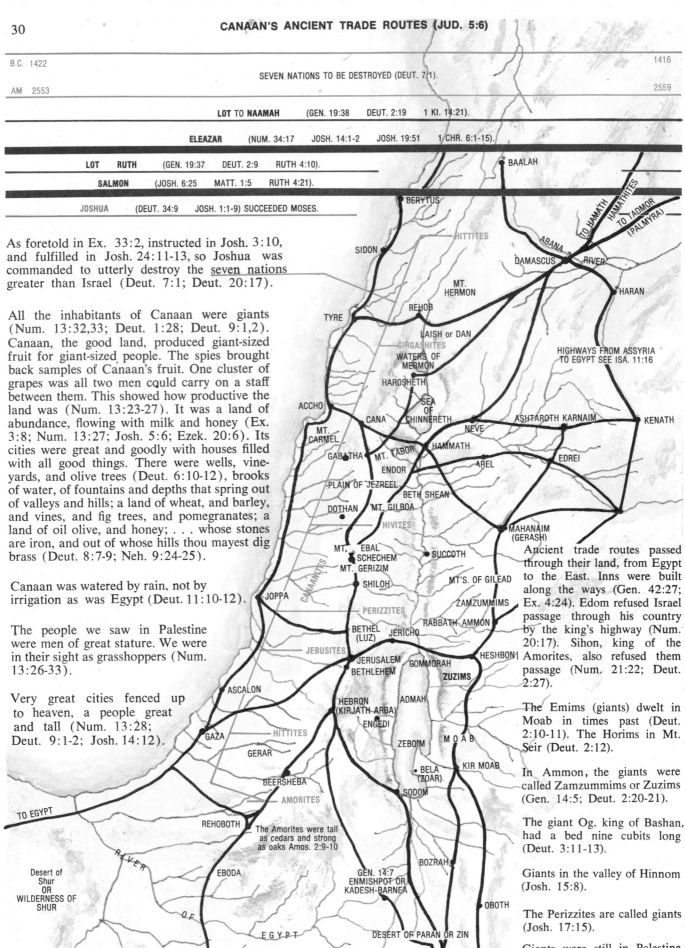

B.C. 1422   1416

AM 2553   2559

SEVEN NATIONS TO BE DESTROYED (DEUT. 7:1).

LOT TO NAAMAH   (GEN. 19:38   DEUT. 2:19   1 KI. 14:21).

ELEAZAR   (NUM. 34:17   JOSH. 14:1-2   JOSH. 19:51   1 CHR. 6:1-15).

LOT   RUTH   (GEN. 19:37   DEUT. 2:9   RUTH 4:10).

SALMON   (JOSH. 6:25   MATT. 1:5   RUTH 4:21).

JOSHUA   (DEUT. 34:9   JOSH. 1:1-9) SUCCEEDED MOSES.

As foretold in Ex. 33:2, instructed in Josh. 3:10, and fulfilled in Josh. 24:11-13, so Joshua was commanded to utterly destroy the seven nations greater than Israel (Deut. 7:1; Deut. 20:17).

All the inhabitants of Canaan were giants (Num. 13:32,33; Deut. 1:28; Deut. 9:1,2). Canaan, the good land, produced giant-sized fruit for giant-sized people. The spies brought back samples of Canaan's fruit. One cluster of grapes was all two men could carry on a staff between them. This showed how productive the land was (Num. 13:23-27). It was a land of abundance, flowing with milk and honey (Ex. 3:8; Num. 13:27; Josh. 5:6; Ezek. 20:6). Its cities were great and goodly with houses filled with all good things. There were wells, vineyards, and olive trees (Deut. 6:10-12), brooks of water, of fountains and depths that spring out of valleys and hills; a land of wheat, and barley, and vines, and fig trees, and pomegranates; a land of oil olive, and honey; . . . whose stones are iron, and out of whose hills thou mayest dig brass (Deut. 8:7-9; Neh. 9:24-25).

Canaan was watered by rain, not by irrigation as was Egypt (Deut. 11:10-12).

The people we saw in Palestine were men of great stature. We were in their sight as grasshoppers (Num. 13:26-33).

Very great cities fenced up to heaven, a people great and tall (Num. 13:28; Deut. 9:1-2; Josh. 14:12).

Ancient trade routes passed through their land, from Egypt to the East. Inns were built along the ways (Gen. 42:27; Ex. 4:24). Edom refused Israel passage through his country by the king's highway (Num. 20:17). Sihon, king of the Amorites, also refused them passage (Num. 21:22; Deut. 2:27).

The Emims (giants) dwelt in Moab in times past (Deut. 2:10-11). The Horims in Mt. Seir (Deut. 2:12).

In Ammon, the giants were called Zamzummims or Zuzims (Gen. 14:5; Deut. 2:20-21).

The giant Og, king of Bashan, had a bed nine cubits long (Deut. 3:11-13).

Giants in the valley of Hinnom (Josh. 15:8).

The Perizzites are called giants (Josh. 17:15).

Giants were still in Palestine in David's time (2 Sam. 21:18-22; 1 Chron. 20:4-8).

The Amorites were tall as cedars and strong as oaks Amos. 2:9-10

THE FIRST SABBATICAL YEAR, SEVENTH YEAR IN CANAAN, ISRAEL'S INHERITANCES WERE ALLOTTED (JOSH. 19:51; 1415 B.C.).

31

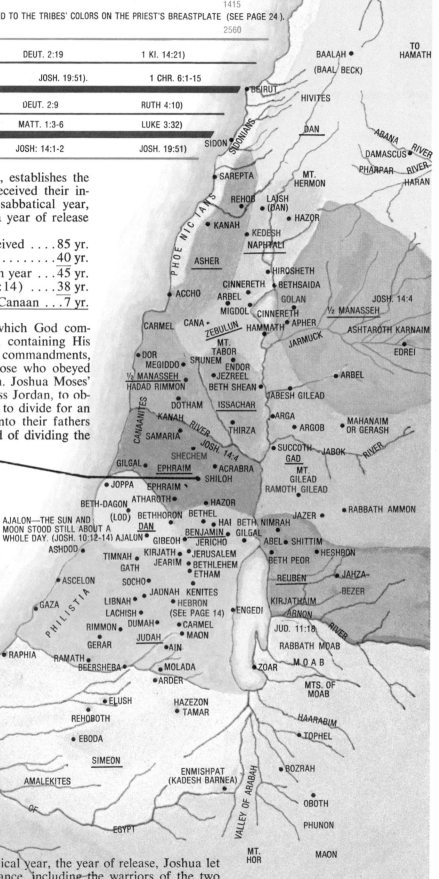

B.C. 1415			1415	
AM 2560		LAND COLORS CORRESPOND TO THE TRIBES' COLORS ON THE PRIEST'S BREASTPLATE (SEE PAGE 24).	2560	
NAAMAH		(GEN. 19:38	DEUT. 2:19	1 KI. 14:21)
ELEAZAR	(NUM. 34:17	JOSH. 14:1-2	JOSH. 19:51).	1 CHR. 6:1-15
RUTH		(GEN. 19:37	DEUT. 2:9	RUTH 4:10)
SALMON		(RUTH 4:18-22	MATT. 1:3-6	LUKE 3:32)
JOSHUA		(NUM. 34:17	JOSH: 14:1-2	JOSH. 19:51)

1415 B.C., Caleb's age (Joshua 14:7-10), establishes the year when the nine and one half tribes received their inheritances. This was during Israel's first sabbatical year, their seventh year in Canaan, which was a year of release (Lev. 25; Deut. 15; 31:10-13).

Caleb's age when the inheritances were received . . . .85 yr.
Caleb's age when he espied out Canaan . . . . .40 yr.
From the espying of Canaan to Caleb's 85th year . . .45 yr.
From Kadesh to the brook Zered (Deut. 2:14) . . . .38 yr.
Deut. 31:9-13, The First year of release in Canaan . . .7 yr.

The book of the law (Deut. 31:9-13), which God commanded Moses, was God's will for man, containing His laws, ways, testimonies, precepts, statutes, commandments, and judgments. God promised to bless those who obeyed them, and curse those who disobeyed them. Joshua Moses' minister, was appointed to lead Israel across Jordan, to observe and do according to all the law, and to divide for an inheritance the land, which God sware unto their fathers to give them. At Shiloh they made an end of dividing the country (Josh. 19:51).

The book of the law was delivered unto the priests the sons of Levi, which bare the ark of the Covenant of the Lord, and unto all the elders of Israel (Deut. 17:8-10; Deut. 31:9).

The priests the Levites, and the judge in Jerusalem must determine the sentence of judgment from the Book of the Law (Deut. 17:8-13). See URIM and THUMMIM (Ex. 28:30; page 24).

A king must copy the Book of the Law, and his copy shall be with him, and he shall read therein all the days of his life (Deut. 17:18-20; 2 KI. 22:8-20; 23:1-25).

1422 B.C. In the year of release, every seven years, this Book of the Law must be read before all Israel (Deut. 31:9-13). Joshua built an altar in Mt. Ebal, when Israel came into Canaan, writing the law of Moses on the stones, and reading them aloud to all Israel and those that were conversant among them (Josh. 8:30-35).

1415 B.C., Seven years later, in the sabbatical year, the year of release, Joshua let the people depart, every man to his inheritance, including the warriors of the two and one-half tribes on the east side of Jordan (Josh. 24:28; Josh. 22:1-6). The law has always been kept in the hearts of believers, even before it was given at Sinai (Heb. 11:1-29; Rom. 4:3; Gal. 3:6-9).

1415 B.C.	1372	1322	1272	1222	1172
	1st JUBILEE	2nd JUBILEE	3rd JUBILEE	4th JUBILEE	5th JUBILEE
	2603	2653	2703	2753	2803

LOT TO **NAAMAH**   THE AMMONITESS, WIFE OF **SOLOMON** (GEN. 19:38; DEUT. 2:19; 1 KI. 14:21).

| ELEAZAR | PHINEHAS (JOSH. 24:33) | **ABISHUA** | **BUKKI** | UZZI   1 CHRON. 6:3-10 | **ZERAHIAH** |

RUTH   (GEN. 19:37   DEUT. 2:9   RUTH 4:13-17).   RUTH

C-1251 B.C.   **OBED**   MATT. 1:5
C-AM 2724

SALMON

THE HARLOT RACHAB (RAHAB)   C-1355 B.C.   **BOAZ**   (RUTH 4:21; MATT. 1:5)   **BOAZ**

JOSHUA

(JOSH. 2; JOSH. 6:25; MATT. 1:5;   C-AM 2620
HEB. 11:31; JAS. 2:25),

MATT. 1:1-6   **SALMON**

TOLA 23

1204 B.C., GIDEON'S 300 WERE VICTORIOUS OVER THE MIDIANITES (JUD. 7:1-25; JUD. 8:1-35).   ABIMELECH [3 YR.]   JUD. 9
1172 B.C.
AM 2803

1212 B.C., THREE DAYS OF FLEECES WHICH GIDEON PUT BEFORE GOD (JUD. 6:36-40)   JERUBBAAL OR   GIDEON 40 YR.

1212 B.C.   [7 YR.]   AM 2771
AM 2763   MIDIANITE (JUD. 6:1-10)

MOSES' RELATIVE KILLS SISERA (JUD. 4:11-21).   DEBORAH AND   BARAK 40 YR.   (JUD. 4:4-24; JUD. 5:1-31)

1252 B.C.   [20 YR.]   JABIN (JUD. 4:13)
AM 2723

SHAMGAR [1 YR.]   (JUD. 3:31)

1332 B.C.   EHUD   80 YR.   (JUD. 3:12-30) LEFT OR RIGHT HANDED
AM 2643

AND IT CAME TO PASS A LONG TIME
AFTER THAT THE LORD HAD GIVEN REST
UNTO ISRAEL . . . JOSHUA CALLED
ALL ISRAEL, AND THEIR ELDERS, HEADS,
JUDGES, AND OFFICERS, . . . JOSH. 23:1,2.
JOSHUA MADE A COVENANT WITH ISRAEL
THAT DAY, AND SET THEM A STATUTE,
AND AN ORDINANCE IN SCHECHEM. ISRAEL
PROMISED TO OBEY THEM (JOSHUA 24:25).

AM 2661
[18] EGLON (JUD. 3:12-14)

OTHNIEL   40 YR.   CALEB'S NEPHEW (JUD. 2:16-19; JUD. 3:9-11).

AM 2621
[8] CHUSHANRISHATHAIM (JUD. 3:1-8)

AM 2613
[10 YR.] THE ELDERS WHO OUTLIVE JOSHUA (JOSH. 24:31; JUD. 2:7).

1372 B.C.
JOSHUA AM 2603   110 YR. OLD ON ISRAEL'S   **FIRST JUBILEE YEAR**   (JOSH. 23:24; JUD. 2:6-10).

JOSHUA LIVED TO CELEBRATE THE FIRST JUBILEE

JOSHUA KEPT ALL THE
FEASTS OF THE LORD (NEH. 8:17; page 23).

JUDGED	FOR	90 YR.

1462 B.C.   **MOSES,** THE JUDGE   FOR 40 YEARS   1422 B.C.   **JOSHUA** AND **ELEAZAR**   JUDGED ISRAEL 50 YEARS   1372 B.C.
AM 2513   (EX. 18:13-27).   (DEUT. 1:15-18).   AM 2553   (NUM. 27:18-23; NUM. 34:17).   (JOSH. 1:4-12; JOSH. 19:51).   AM 2603

(SEE PAGE 22)   (SEE PAGE 28)   (DEUT. 31:7)

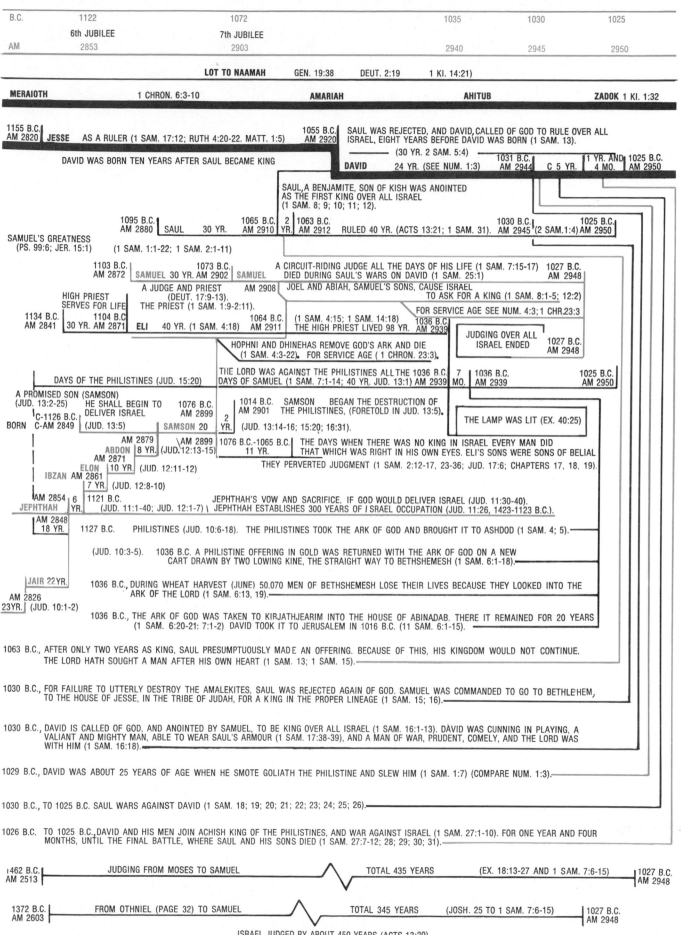

B.C.	1122	1072	1035	1030	1025
	6th JUBILEE	7th JUBILEE			
AM	2853	2903	2940	2945	2950

LOT TO NAAMAH   GEN. 19:38   DEUT. 2:19   1 KI. 14:21)

MERAIOTH   1 CHRON. 6:3-10   **AMARIAH**   **AHITUB**   **ZADOK** 1 KI. 1:32

1155 B.C.
AM 2820   **JESSE**   AS A RULER (1 SAM. 17:12; RUTH 4:20-22. MATT. 1:5)   1055 B.C.
AM 2920   SAUL WAS REJECTED, AND DAVID, CALLED OF GOD TO RULE OVER ALL
ISRAEL, EIGHT YEARS BEFORE DAVID WAS BORN (1 SAM. 13).

DAVID WAS BORN TEN YEARS AFTER SAUL BECAME KING   — (30 YR. 2 SAM. 5:4) —   1031 B.C.   1 YR. AND 1025 B.C.
DAVID   24 YR. (SEE NUM. 1:3)   AM 2944   C 5 YR.   4 MO.   AM 2950

SAUL, A BENJAMITE, SON OF KISH WAS ANOINTED
AS THE FIRST KING OVER ALL ISRAEL
(1 SAM. 8; 9; 10; 11; 12).

1095 B.C.   1065 B.C. 2   1063 B.C.   1030 B.C.   1025 B.C.
AM 2880   **SAUL**   30 YR.   AM 2910 YR. AM 2912   RULED 40 YR. (ACTS 13:21; 1 SAM. 31).   AM 2945 (2 SAM.1:4) AM 2950

SAMUEL'S GREATNESS
(PS. 99:6; JER. 15:1)   (1 SAM. 1:1-22; 1 SAM. 2:1-11)

1103 B.C.   1073 B.C.   A CIRCUIT-RIDING JUDGE ALL THE DAYS OF HIS LIFE (1 SAM. 7:15-17)   1027 B.C.
AM 2872   **SAMUEL** 30 YR. AM 2902   **SAMUEL**   DIED DURING SAUL'S WARS ON DAVID (1 SAM. 25:1)   AM 2948
AM 2908   JOEL AND ABIAH, SAMUEL'S SONS, CAUSE ISRAEL

A JUDGE AND PRIEST   TO ASK FOR A KING (1 SAM. 8:1-5; 12:2)
HIGH PRIEST   (DEUT. 17:9-13).   FOR SERVICE AGE SEE NUM. 4:3; 1 CHR.23:3
SERVES FOR LIFE   THE PRIEST (1 SAM. 1:9-2:11).
1134 B.C.   1104 B.C   1064 B.C.   (1 SAM. 4:15; 1 SAM. 14:18)   1036 B.C.   JUDGING OVER ALL   1027 B.C.
AM 2841   30 YR. AM 2871   **ELI**   40 YR. (1 SAM. 4:18)   AM 2911   THE HIGH PRIEST LIVED 98 YR. AM 2939   ISRAEL ENDED   AM 2948

HOPHNI AND DHINEHAS REMOVE GOD'S ARK AND DIE
(1 SAM. 4:3-22). FOR SERVICE AGE (1 CHRON. 23:3).

DAYS OF THE PHILISTINES (JUD. 15:20)   THE LORD WAS AGAINST THE PHILISTINES ALL THE 1036 B.C. 7   1036 B.C.   1025 B.C.
DAYS OF SAMUEL (1 SAM. 7:1-14; 40 YR. JUD. 13:1) AM 2939 MO.   AM 2939   AM 2950

A PROMISED SON (SAMSON)
(JUD. 13:2-25)   HE SHALL BEGIN TO   1076 B.C.   1014 B.C.   SAMSON   BEGAN THE DESTRUCTION OF
C-1126 B.C.   DELIVER ISRAEL   AM 2899   AM 2901   THE PHILISTINES, (FORETOLD IN JUD. 13:5).   THE LAMP WAS LIT (EX. 40:25)
BORN   C-AM 2849   (JUD. 13:5)   **SAMSON** 20   2   (JUD. 13:14-16; 15:20; 16:31).
YR.

AM 2879   AM 2899   1076 B.C.-1065 B.C.   THE DAYS WHEN THERE WAS NO KING IN ISRAEL EVERY MAN DID
ABDON 8 YR. (JUD.12:13-15)   11 YR.   THAT WHICH WAS RIGHT IN HIS OWN EYES. ELI'S SONS WERE SONS OF BELIAL
AM 2871   THEY PERVERTED JUDGMENT (1 SAM. 2:12-17, 23-36; JUD. 17:6; CHAPTERS 17, 18, 19).
ELON 10 YR. (JUD. 12:11-12)
IBZAN AM 2861
7 YR. (JUD. 12:8-10)
AM 2854 6   1121 B.C.   JEPHTHAH'S VOW AND SACRIFICE, IF GOD WOULD DELIVER ISRAEL (JUD. 11:30-40).
JEPHTHAH YR.   (JUD. 11:1-40; JUD. 12:1-7)   JEPHTHAH ESTABLISHES 300 YEARS OF ISRAEL OCCUPATION (JUD. 11:26, 1423-1123 B.C.).
AM 2848
18 YR.   1127 B.C.   PHILISTINES (JUD. 10:6-18). THE PHILISTINES TOOK THE ARK OF GOD AND BROUGHT IT TO ASHDOD (1 SAM. 4; 5).

(JUD. 10:3-5).   1036 B.C. A PHILISTINE OFFERING IN GOLD WAS RETURNED WITH THE ARK OF GOD ON A NEW
CART DRAWN BY TWO LOWING KINE, THE STRAIGHT WAY TO BETHSHEMESH (1 SAM. 6:1-18).

JAIR 22YR.   1036 B.C., DURING WHEAT HARVEST (JUNE) 50.070 MEN OF BETHSHEMESH LOSE THEIR LIVES BECAUSE THEY LOOKED INTO THE
AM 2826   ARK OF THE LORD (1 SAM. 6:13, 19).
23YR. (JUD. 10:1-2)
1036 B.C., THE ARK OF GOD WAS TAKEN TO KIRJATHJEARIM INTO THE HOUSE OF ABINADAB. THERE IT REMAINED FOR 20 YEARS
(1 SAM. 6:20-21: 7:1-2) DAVID TOOK IT TO JERUSALEM IN 1016 B.C. (11 SAM. 6:1-15).

1063 B.C., AFTER ONLY TWO YEARS AS KING, SAUL PRESUMPTUOUSLY MADE AN OFFERING. BECAUSE OF THIS, HIS KINGDOM WOULD NOT CONTINUE.
THE LORD HATH SOUGHT A MAN AFTER HIS OWN HEART (1 SAM. 13; 1 SAM. 15).

1030 B.C., FOR FAILURE TO UTTERLY DESTROY THE AMALEKITES, SAUL WAS REJECTED AGAIN OF GOD. SAMUEL WAS COMMANDED TO GO TO BETHLEHEM,
TO THE HOUSE OF JESSE, IN THE TRIBE OF JUDAH, FOR A KING IN THE PROPER LINEAGE (1 SAM. 15; 16).

1030 B.C., DAVID IS CALLED OF GOD, AND ANOINTED BY SAMUEL, TO BE KING OVER ALL ISRAEL (1 SAM. 16:1-13). DAVID WAS CUNNING IN PLAYING, A
VALIANT AND MIGHTY MAN, ABLE TO WEAR SAUL'S ARMOUR (1 SAM. 17:38-39), AND A MAN OF WAR, PRUDENT, COMELY, AND THE LORD WAS
WITH HIM (1 SAM. 16:18).

1029 B.C., DAVID WAS ABOUT 25 YEARS OF AGE WHEN HE SMOTE GOLIATH THE PHILISTINE AND SLEW HIM (1 SAM. 1:7) (COMPARE NUM. 1:3).

1030 B.C., TO 1025 B.C. SAUL WARS AGAINST DAVID (1 SAM. 18; 19; 20; 21; 22; 23; 24; 25; 26).

1026 B.C. TO 1025 B.C.,DAVID AND HIS MEN JOIN ACHISH KING OF THE PHILISTINES, AND WAR AGAINST ISRAEL (1 SAM. 27:1-10). FOR ONE YEAR AND FOUR
MONTHS, UNTIL THE FINAL BATTLE, WHERE SAUL AND HIS SONS DIED (1 SAM. 27:7-12; 28; 29; 30; 31).

1462 B.C.   JUDGING FROM MOSES TO SAMUEL   TOTAL 435 YEARS   (EX. 18:13-27 AND 1 SAM. 7:6-15)   1027 B.C.
AM 2513   AM 2948

1372 B.C.   FROM OTHNIEL (PAGE 32) TO SAMUEL   TOTAL 345 YEARS   (JOSH. 25 TO 1 SAM. 7:6-15)   1027 B.C.
AM 2603   AM 2948

ISRAEL, JUDGED BY ABOUT 450 YEARS (ACTS 13:20).

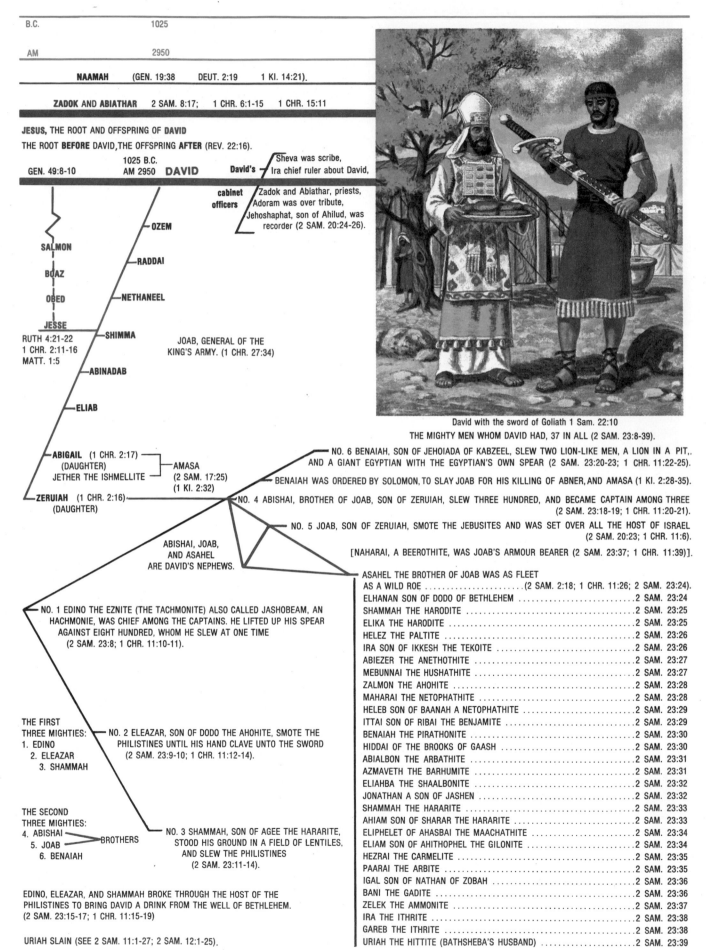

B.C.   1025

AM   2950

NAAMAH   (GEN. 19:38   DEUT. 2:19   1 KI. 14:21).

ZADOK AND **ABIATHAR**   2 SAM. 8:17;   1 CHR. 6:1-15   1 CHR. 15:11

JESUS, THE ROOT AND OFFSPRING OF DAVID

THE ROOT **BEFORE** DAVID, THE OFFSPRING **AFTER** (REV. 22:16).

GEN. 49:8-10   1025 B.C.

AM 2950   **DAVID**

David's

cabinet officers

Sheva was scribe, Ira chief ruler about David,

Zadok and Abiathar, priests, Adoram was over tribute, Jehoshaphat, son of Ahilud, was recorder (2 SAM. 20:24-26).

SALMON

BOAZ

OBED

JESSE

RUTH 4:21-22
1 CHR. 2:11-16
MATT. 1:5

— OZEM

— RADDAI

— NETHANEEL

— SHIMMA   JOAB, GENERAL OF THE KING'S ARMY. (1 CHR. 27:34)

— ABINADAB

— ELIAB

— **ABIGAIL** (1 CHR. 2:17)
(DAUGHTER)
JETHER THE ISHMELLITE

AMASA
(2 SAM. 17:25)
(1 KI. 2:32)

— **ZERUIAH** (1 CHR. 2:16)
(DAUGHTER)

ABISHAI, JOAB, AND ASAHEL ARE DAVID'S NEPHEWS.

NO. 6 BENAIAH, SON OF JEHOIADA OF KABZEEL, SLEW TWO LION-LIKE MEN, A LION IN A PIT, AND A GIANT EGYPTIAN WITH THE EGYPTIAN'S OWN SPEAR (2 SAM. 23:20-23; 1 CHR. 11:22-25).

BENAIAH WAS ORDERED BY SOLOMON, TO SLAY JOAB FOR HIS KILLING OF ABNER, AND AMASA (1 KI. 2:28-35).

NO. 4 ABISHAI, BROTHER OF JOAB, SON OF ZERUIAH, SLEW THREE HUNDRED, AND BECAME CAPTAIN AMONG THREE (2 SAM. 23:18-19; 1 CHR. 11:20-21).

NO. 5 JOAB, SON OF ZERUIAH, SMOTE THE JEBUSITES AND WAS SET OVER ALL THE HOST OF ISRAEL (2 SAM. 20:23; 1 CHR. 11:6).

[NAHARAI, A BEEROTHITE, WAS JOAB'S ARMOUR BEARER (2 SAM. 23:37; 1 CHR. 11:39)].

NO. 1 EDINO THE EZNITE (THE TACHMONITE) ALSO CALLED JASHOBEAM, AN HACHMONIE, WAS CHIEF AMONG THE CAPTAINS. HE LIFTED UP HIS SPEAR AGAINST EIGHT HUNDRED, WHOM HE SLEW AT ONE TIME (2 SAM. 23:8; 1 CHR. 11:10-11).

THE FIRST THREE MIGHTIES:
1. EDINO
2. ELEAZAR
3. SHAMMAH

NO. 2 ELEAZAR, SON OF DODO THE AHOHITE, SMOTE THE PHILISTINES UNTIL HIS HAND CLAVE UNTO THE SWORD (2 SAM. 23:9-10; 1 CHR. 11:12-14).

THE SECOND THREE MIGHTIES:
4. ABISHAI
5. JOAB   BROTHERS
6. BENAIAH

NO. 3 SHAMMAH, SON OF AGEE THE HARARITE, STOOD HIS GROUND IN A FIELD OF LENTILES, AND SLEW THE PHILISTINES (2 SAM. 23:11-14).

EDINO, ELEAZAR, AND SHAMMAH BROKE THROUGH THE HOST OF THE PHILISTINES TO BRING DAVID A DRINK FROM THE WELL OF BETHLEHEM. (2 SAM. 23:15-17; 1 CHR. 11:15-19)

URIAH SLAIN (SEE 2 SAM. 11:1-27; 2 SAM. 12:1-25).

David with the sword of Goliath 1 Sam. 22:10

THE MIGHTY MEN WHOM DAVID HAD, 37 IN ALL (2 SAM. 23:8-39).

ASAHEL THE BROTHER OF JOAB WAS AS FLEET
AS A WILD ROE .... (2 SAM. 2:18; 1 CHR. 11:26; 2 SAM. 23:24).
ELHANAN SON OF DODO OF BETHLEHEM .... 2 SAM. 23:24
SHAMMAH THE HARODITE .... 2 SAM. 23:25
ELIKA THE HARODITE .... 2 SAM. 23:25
HELEZ THE PALTITE .... 2 SAM. 23:26
IRA SON OF IKKESH THE TEKOITE .... 2 SAM. 23:26
ABIEZER THE ANETHOTHITE .... 2 SAM. 23:27
MEBUNNAI THE HUSHATHITE .... 2 SAM. 23:27
ZALMON THE AHOHITE .... 2 SAM. 23:28
MAHARAI THE NETOPHATHITE .... 2 SAM. 23:28
HELEB SON OF BAANAH A NETOPHATHITE .... 2 SAM. 23:29
ITTAI SON OF RIBAI THE BENJAMITE .... 2 SAM. 23:29
BENAIAH THE PIRATHONITE .... 2 SAM. 23:30
HIDDAI OF THE BROOKS OF GAASH .... 2 SAM. 23:30
ABIALBON THE ARBATHITE .... 2 SAM. 23:31
AZMAVETH THE BARHUMITE .... 2 SAM. 23:31
ELIAHBA THE SHAALBONITE .... 2 SAM. 23:32
JONATHAN A SON OF JASHEN .... 2 SAM. 23:32
SHAMMAH THE HARARITE .... 2 SAM. 23:33
AHIAM SON OF SHARAR THE HARARITE .... 2 SAM. 23:33
ELIPHELET OF AHASBAI THE MAACHATHITE .... 2 SAM. 23:34
ELIAM SON OF AHITHOPHEL THE GILONITE .... 2 SAM. 23:34
HEZRAI THE CARMELITE .... 2 SAM. 23:35
PAARAI THE ARBITE .... 2 SAM. 23:35
IGAL SON OF NATHAN OF ZOBAH .... 2 SAM. 23:36
BANI THE GADITE .... 2 SAM. 23:36
ZELEK THE AMMONITE .... 2 SAM. 23:37
IRA THE ITHRITE .... 2 SAM. 23:38
GAREB THE ITHRITE .... 2 SAM. 23:38
URIAH THE HITTITE (BATHSHEBA'S HUSBAND) .... 2 SAM. 23:39

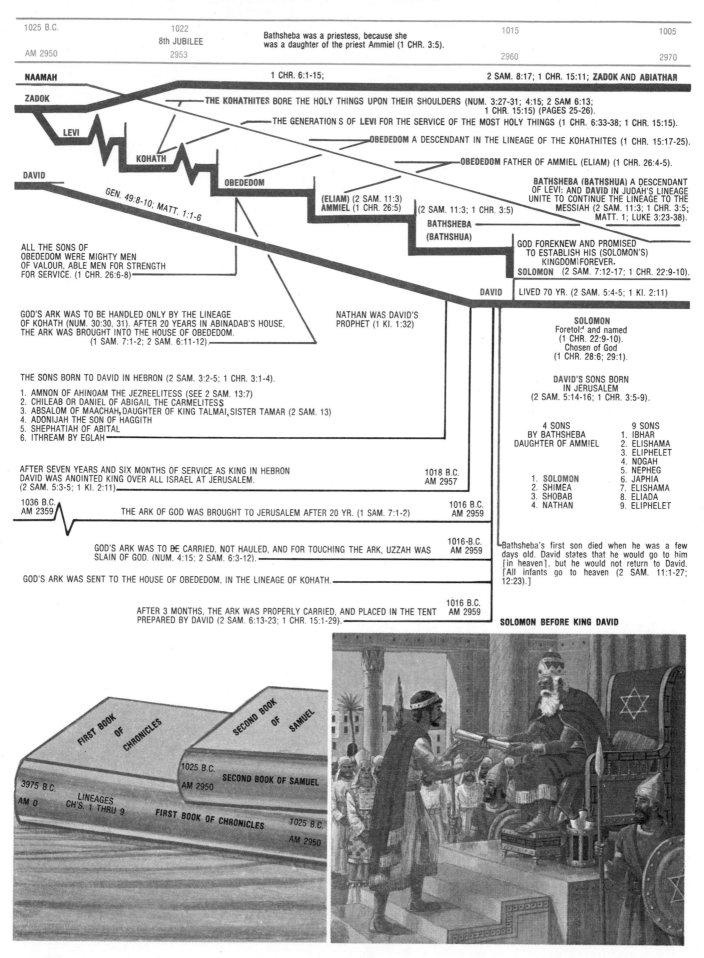

1025 B.C.   1022   1015   1005
                             8th JUBILEE
AM 2950   2953   Bathsheba was a priestess, because she   2960   2970
                                          was a daughter of the priest Ammiel (1 CHR. 3:5).

NAAMAH   1 CHR. 6:1-15;   2 SAM. 8:17; 1 CHR. 15:11; **ZADOK** AND **ABIATHAR**

ZADOK
                        THE KOHATHITES BORE THE HOLY THINGS UPON THEIR SHOULDERS (NUM. 3:27-31; 4:15; 2 SAM 6:13;
                                                                              1 CHR. 15:15) (PAGES 25-26).
        LEVI   THE GENERATIONS OF **LEVI** FOR THE SERVICE OF THE MOST HOLY THINGS (1 CHR. 6:33-38; 1 CHR. 15:15).

                KOHATH   **OBEDEDOM** A DESCENDANT IN THE LINEAGE OF THE KOHATHITES (1 CHR. 15:17-25).

DAVID   **OBEDEDOM** FATHER OF AMMIEL (ELIAM) (1 CHR. 26:4-5).

                         OBEDEDOM   **BATHSHEBA (BATHSHUA)** A DESCENDANT
                                                                                         OF LEVI; AND **DAVID** IN JUDAH'S LINEAGE
            GEN. 49:8-10; MATT. 1:1-6   **(ELIAM)** (2 SAM. 11:3)   UNITE TO CONTINUE THE LINEAGE TO THE
                                             AMMIEL (1 CHR. 26:5)   MESSIAH (2 SAM. 11:3; 1 CHR. 3:5;
                                                              (2 SAM. 11:3; 1 CHR. 3:5) MATT. 1; LUKE 3:23-38).

                                                                        BATHSHEBA
                                                                        (BATHSHUA)
ALL THE SONS OF   GOD FOREKNEW AND PROMISED
OBEDEDOM WERE MIGHTY MEN   TO ESTABLISH HIS (SOLOMON'S)
OF VALOUR, ABLE MEN FOR STRENGTH   KINGDOM FOREVER.
FOR SERVICE. (1 CHR. 26:6-8)   **SOLOMON** (2 SAM. 7:12-17; 1 CHR. 22:9-10).

                                                              DAVID   LIVED 70 YR. (2 SAM. 5:4-5; 1 KI. 2:11)

GOD'S ARK WAS TO BE HANDLED ONLY BY THE LINEAGE   NATHAN WAS DAVID'S   **SOLOMON**
OF KOHATH (NUM. 30:30, 31). AFTER 20 YEARS IN ABINADAB'S HOUSE,   PROPHET (1 KI. 1:32)   Foretold and named
THE ARK WAS BROUGHT INTO THE HOUSE OF OBEDEDOM.   (1 CHR. 22:9-10).
         (1 SAM. 7:1-2; 2 SAM. 6:11-12).   Chosen of God
                                                                                                (1 CHR. 28:6; 29:1).

THE SONS BORN TO DAVID IN HEBRON (2 SAM. 3:2-5; 1 CHR. 3:1-4).   DAVID'S SONS BORN
                                                                                                IN JERUSALEM
1. AMNON OF AHINOAM THE JEZREELITESS (SEE 2 SAM. 13:7)   (2 SAM. 5:14-16; 1 CHR. 3:5-9).
2. CHILEAB OR DANIEL OF ABIGAIL THE CARMELITESS
3. ABSALOM OF MAACHAH, DAUGHTER OF KING TALMAI, SISTER TAMAR (2 SAM. 13)   4 SONS   9 SONS
4. ADONIJAH THE SON OF HAGGITH   BY BATHSHEBA   1. IBHAR
5. SHEPHATIAH OF ABITAL   DAUGHTER OF AMMIEL   2. ELISHAMA
6. ITHREAM BY EGLAH   3. ELIPHELET
                                                                                                  4. NOGAH
                                                                                                  5. NEPHEG
                                                                            1. SOLOMON   6. JAPHIA
AFTER SEVEN YEARS AND SIX MONTHS OF SERVICE AS KING IN HEBRON   2. SHIMEA   7. ELISHAMA
DAVID WAS ANOINTED KING OVER ALL ISRAEL AT JERUSALEM.   1018 B.C.   3. SHOBAB   8. ELIADA
(2 SAM. 5:3-5; 1 KI. 2:11)   AM 2957   4. NATHAN   9. ELIPHELET

1036 B.C.   1016 B.C.
AM 2359   THE ARK OF GOD WAS BROUGHT TO JERUSALEM AFTER 20 YR. (1 SAM. 7:1-2)   AM 2959

                                                            1016 B.C.
GOD'S ARK WAS TO BE CARRIED, NOT HAULED, AND FOR TOUCHING THE ARK, UZZAH WAS   AM 2959   Bathsheba's first son died when he was a few
SLAIN OF GOD. (NUM. 4:15; 2 SAM. 6:3-12).   days old. David states that he would go to him
                                                                                          [in heaven], but he would not return to David.
GOD'S ARK WAS SENT TO THE HOUSE OF OBEDEDOM, IN THE LINEAGE OF KOHATH.   [All infants go to heaven (2 SAM. 11:1-27;
                                                                                          12:23).]
                                                            1016 B.C.
AFTER 3 MONTHS, THE ARK WAS PROPERLY CARRIED, AND PLACED IN THE TENT   AM 2959
PREPARED BY DAVID (2 SAM. 6:13-23; 1 CHR. 15:1-29).   **SOLOMON BEFORE KING DAVID**

FIRST BOOK OF CHRONICLES   SECOND BOOK OF SAMUEL

                        1025 B.C.
                        AM 2950   SECOND BOOK OF SAMUEL

3975 B.C.
AM 0   LINEAGES
            CH'S. 1 THRU 9   FIRST BOOK OF CHRONICLES   1025 B.C.
                                                           AM 2950

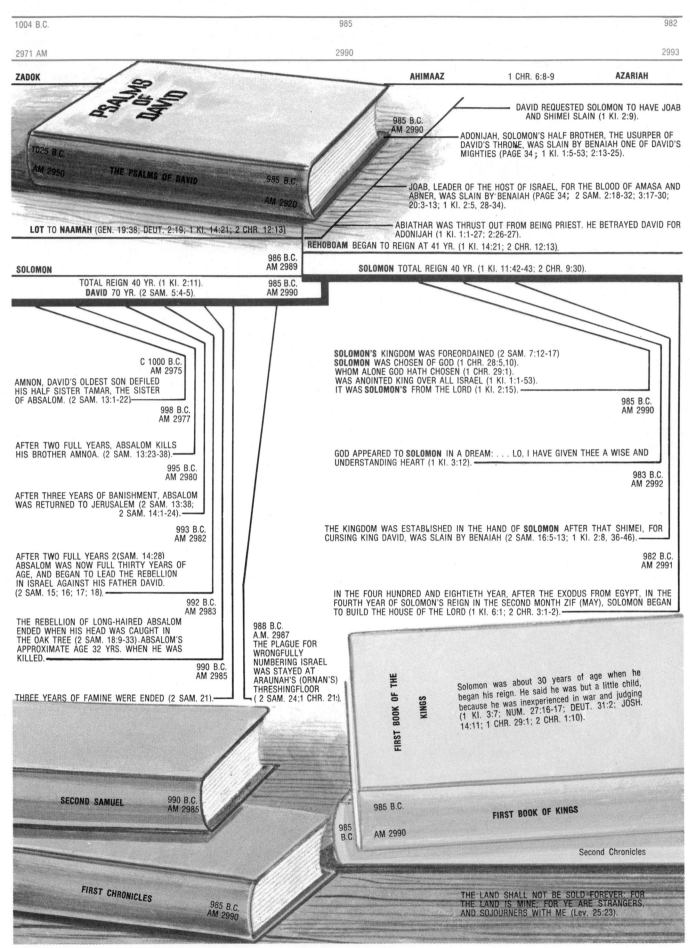

1004 B.C.   985   982

2971 AM   2990   2993

ZADOK   **AHIMAAZ**   1 CHR. 6:8-9   **AZARIAH**

PSALMS OF DAVID

1025 B.C.
AM 2950
THE PSALMS OF DAVID

985 B.C.

AM 2920

985 B.C.
AM 2990

DAVID REQUESTED SOLOMON TO HAVE JOAB AND SHIMEI SLAIN (1 KI. 2:9).

ADONIJAH, SOLOMON'S HALF BROTHER, THE USURPER OF DAVID'S THRONE, WAS SLAIN BY BENAIAH ONE OF DAVID'S MIGHTIES (PAGE 34; 1 KI. 1:5-53; 2:13-25).

JOAB, LEADER OF THE HOST OF ISRAEL, FOR THE BLOOD OF AMASA AND ABNER, WAS SLAIN BY BENAIAH (PAGE 34; 2 SAM. 2:18-32; 3:17-30; 20:3-13; 1 KI. 2:5, 28-34).

ABIATHAR WAS THRUST OUT FROM BEING PRIEST. HE BETRAYED DAVID FOR ADONIJAH (1 KI. 1:1-27; 2:26-27).

LOT TO **NAAMAH** (GEN. 19:38; DEUT. 2:19; 1 KI. 14:21; 2 CHR. 12:13)

REHOBOAM BEGAN TO REIGN AT 41 YR. (1 KI. 14:21; 2 CHR. 12:13).

SOLOMON

986 B.C.
AM 2989

985 B.C.
AM 2990

SOLOMON TOTAL REIGN 40 YR. (1 KI. 11:42-43; 2 CHR. 9:30).

TOTAL REIGN 40 YR. (1 KI. 2:11).
DAVID 70 YR. (2 SAM. 5:4-5).

C 1000 B.C.
AM 2975

AMNON, DAVID'S OLDEST SON DEFILED HIS HALF SISTER TAMAR, THE SISTER OF ABSALOM. (2 SAM. 13:1-22)

998 B.C.
AM 2977

AFTER TWO FULL YEARS, ABSALOM KILLS HIS BROTHER AMNOA. (2 SAM. 13:23-38).

995 B.C.
AM 2980

AFTER THREE YEARS OF BANISHMENT, ABSALOM WAS RETURNED TO JERUSALEM (2 SAM. 13:38; 2 SAM. 14:1-24).

993 B.C.
AM 2982

AFTER TWO FULL YEARS 2(SAM. 14:28) ABSALOM WAS NOW FULL THIRTY YEARS OF AGE, AND BEGAN TO LEAD THE REBELLION IN ISRAEL AGAINST HIS FATHER DAVID. (2 SAM. 15; 16; 17; 18).

992 B.C.
AM 2983

THE REBELLION OF LONG-HAIRED ABSALOM ENDED WHEN HIS HEAD WAS CAUGHT IN THE OAK TREE (2 SAM. 18:9-33). ABSALOM'S APPROXIMATE AGE 32 YRS. WHEN HE WAS KILLED.

990 B.C.
AM 2985

THREE YEARS OF FAMINE WERE ENDED (2 SAM. 21).

SOLOMON'S KINGDOM WAS FOREORDAINED (2 SAM. 7:12-17)
SOLOMON WAS CHOSEN OF GOD (1 CHR. 28:5,10).
WHOM ALONE GOD HATH CHOSEN (1 CHR. 29:1).
WAS ANOINTED KING OVER ALL ISRAEL (1 KI. 1:1-53).
IT WAS **SOLOMON'S** FROM THE LORD (1 KI. 2:15).

985 B.C.
AM 2990

GOD APPEARED TO **SOLOMON** IN A DREAM: . . . LO, I HAVE GIVEN THEE A WISE AND UNDERSTANDING HEART (1 KI. 3:12).

983 B.C.
AM 2992

THE KINGDOM WAS ESTABLISHED IN THE HAND OF **SOLOMON** AFTER THAT SHIMEI, FOR CURSING KING DAVID, WAS SLAIN BY BENAIAH (2 SAM. 16:5-13; 1 KI. 2:8, 36-46).

982 B.C.
AM 2991

IN THE FOUR HUNDRED AND EIGHTIETH YEAR, AFTER THE EXODUS FROM EGYPT, IN THE FOURTH YEAR OF SOLOMON'S REIGN IN THE SECOND MONTH ZIF (MAY), SOLOMON BEGAN TO BUILD THE HOUSE OF THE LORD (1 KI. 6:1; 2 CHR. 3:1-2).

988 B.C.
A.M. 2987
THE PLAGUE FOR WRONGFULLY NUMBERING ISRAEL WAS STAYED AT ARAUNAH'S (ORNAN'S) THRESHINGFLOOR (2 SAM. 24;1 CHR. 21:).

FIRST BOOK OF THE KINGS

Solomon was about 30 years of age when he began his reign. He said he was but a little child, because he was inexperienced in war and judging (1 KI. 3:7; NUM. 27:16-17; DEUT. 31:2; JOSH. 14:11; 1 CHR. 29:1; 2 CHR. 1:10).

SECOND SAMUEL   990 B.C.
AM 2985

985 B.C.
AM 2990
FIRST BOOK OF KINGS

985
B.C.

Second Chronicles

FIRST CHRONICLES   985 B.C.
AM 2990

THE LAND SHALL NOT BE SOLD FOREVER: FOR THE LAND IS MINE; FOR YE ARE STRANGERS, AND SOJOURNERS WITH ME (Lev. 25:23).

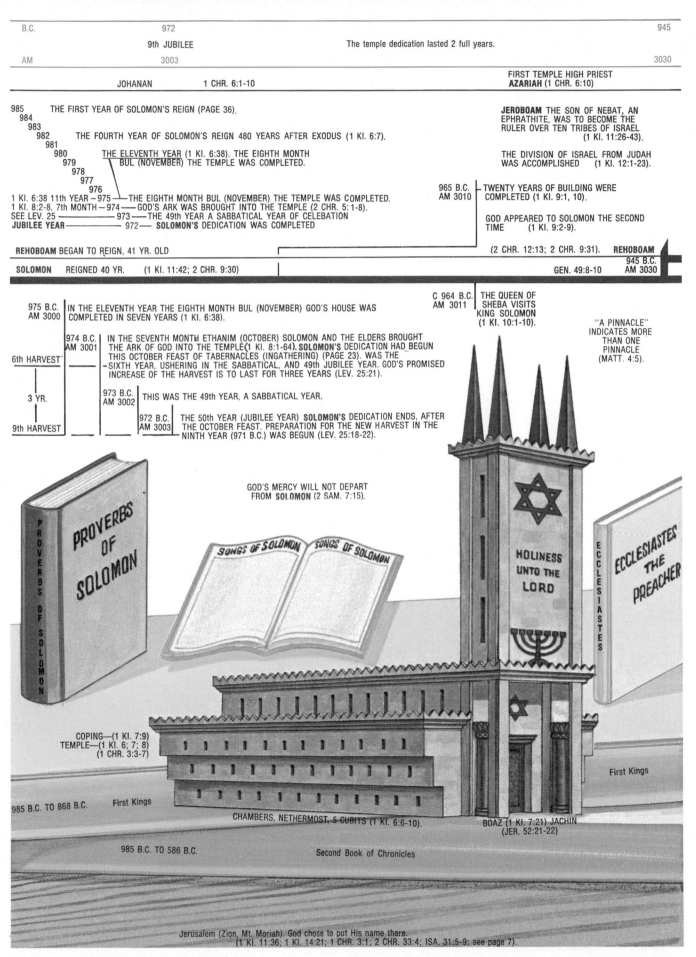

B.C.   972   945

9th JUBILEE   The temple dedication lasted 2 full years.

AM   3003   3030

JOHANAN   1 CHR. 6:1-10

FIRST TEMPLE HIGH PRIEST
AZARIAH (1 CHR. 6:10)

985   THE FIRST YEAR OF SOLOMON'S REIGN (PAGE 36).
984
983
982   THE FOURTH YEAR OF SOLOMON'S REIGN 480 YEARS AFTER EXODUS (1 KI. 6:7).
981
980   THE ELEVENTH YEAR (1 KI. 6:38). THE EIGHTH MONTH
979   BUL (NOVEMBER) THE TEMPLE WAS COMPLETED.
978
977
976
1 KI. 6:38 11th YEAR – 975 —— THE EIGHTH MONTH BUL (NOVEMBER) THE TEMPLE WAS COMPLETED.
1 KI. 8:2-8, 7th MONTH – 974 —— GOD'S ARK WAS BROUGHT INTO THE TEMPLE (2 CHR. 5:1-8).
SEE LEV. 25 —————— 973 —— THE 49th YEAR A SABBATICAL YEAR OF CELEBATION
JUBILEE YEAR —————— 972 —— **SOLOMON'S** DEDICATION WAS COMPLETED

REHOBOAM BEGAN TO REIGN, 41 YR. OLD

SOLOMON   REIGNED 40 YR.   (1 KI. 11:42; 2 CHR. 9:30)

JEROBOAM THE SON OF NEBAT, AN
EPHRATHITE, WAS TO BECOME THE
RULER OVER TEN TRIBES OF ISRAEL
(1 KI. 11:26-43).

THE DIVISION OF ISRAEL FROM JUDAH
WAS ACCOMPLISHED   (1 KI. 12:1-23).

965 B.C. — TWENTY YEARS OF BUILDING WERE
AM 3010   COMPLETED (1 KI. 9:1, 10).

GOD APPEARED TO SOLOMON THE SECOND
TIME   (1 KI. 9:2-9).

(2 CHR. 12:13; 2 CHR. 9:31).   **REHOBOAM**

945 B.C.
GEN. 49:8-10   AM 3030

975 B.C.   IN THE ELEVENTH YEAR THE EIGHTH MONTH BUL (NOVEMBER) GOD'S HOUSE WAS
AM 3000   COMPLETED IN SEVEN YEARS (1 KI. 6:38).

974 B.C.   IN THE SEVENTH MONTH ETHANIM (OCTOBER) SOLOMON AND THE ELDERS BROUGHT
AM 3001   THE ARK OF GOD INTO THE TEMPLE (1 KI. 8:1-64). **SOLOMON'S** DEDICATION HAD BEGUN
   THIS OCTOBER FEAST OF TABERNACLES (INGATHERING) (PAGE 23). WAS THE
6th HARVEST   –SIXTH YEAR, USHERING IN THE SABBATICAL, AND 49th JUBILEE YEAR. GOD'S PROMISED
   INCREASE OF THE HARVEST IS TO LAST FOR THREE YEARS (LEV. 25:21).

3 YR.   973 B.C.   THIS WAS THE 49th YEAR, A SABBATICAL YEAR.
   AM 3002

9th HARVEST   972 B.C.   THE 50th YEAR (JUBILEE YEAR) **SOLOMON'S** DEDICATION ENDS, AFTER
   AM 3003   THE OCTOBER FEAST. PREPARATION FOR THE NEW HARVEST IN THE
   NINTH YEAR (971 B.C.) WAS BEGUN (LEV. 25:18-22).

C 964 B.C.   THE QUEEN OF
AM 3011   SHEBA VISITS
   KING SOLOMON
   (1 KI. 10:1-10).

"A PINNACLE"
INDICATES MORE
THAN ONE
PINNACLE
(MATT. 4:5).

PROVERBS OF SOLOMON

SONGS OF SOLOMON   SONGS OF SOLOMON

GOD'S MERCY WILL NOT DEPART
FROM **SOLOMON** (2 SAM. 7:15).

HOLINESS UNTO THE LORD

ECCLESIASTES

ECCLESIASTES THE PREACHER

First Kings

COPING—(1 KI. 7:9)
TEMPLE—(1 KI. 6; 7; 8)
(1 CHR. 3:3-7)

985 B.C. TO 868 B.C.   First Kings

CHAMBERS, NETHERMOST, 5 CUBITS (1 KI. 6:6-10).

BOAZ (1 KI. 7:21) JACHIN
(JER. 52:21-22)

985 B.C. TO 586 B.C.   Second Book of Chronicles

Jerusalem (Zion, Mt. Moriah). God chose to put His name there.
(1 KI. 11:36; 1 KI. 14:21; 1 CHR. 3:1; 2 CHR. 33:4; ISA. 31:5-9; see page 7).

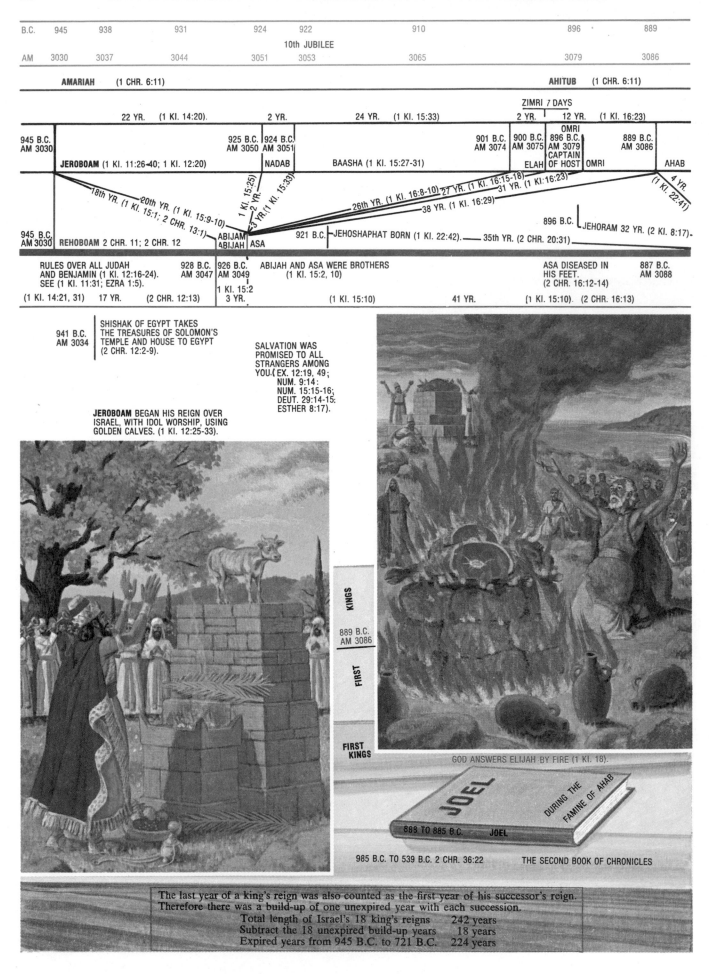

B.C.	945	938	931	924	922	910	896	889
					10th JUBILEE			
AM	3030	3037	3044	3051	3053	3065	3079	3086

AMARIAH (1 CHR. 6:11)   **AHITUB** (1 CHR. 6:11)

ZIMRI 7 DAYS

22 YR. (1 KI. 14:20).   2 YR.   24 YR. (1 KI. 15:33)   2 YR.   12 YR. (1 KI. 16:23)

945 B.C. AM 3030   925 B.C. AM 3050   924 B.C. AM 3051   901 B.C. AM 3074   900 B.C. AM 3075   OMRI 896 B.C. AM 3079 CAPTAIN OF HOST   889 B.C. AM 3086

JEROBOAM (1 KI. 11:26-40; 1 KI. 12:20)   NADAB   BAASHA (1 KI. 15:27-31)   ELAH   OMRI   AHAB

18th YR. (1 KI. 15:1; 2 CHR. 13:1)   20th YR. (1 KI. 15:9-10)   1 KI. 15:25)   2 YR. (1 KI. 15:33)   26th YR. (1 KI. 16:8-10)   27 YR. (1 KI. 16:15-18)   31 YR. (1 KI. 16:23)   38 YR. (1 KI. 16:29)   4 YR. (1 KI. 22:41)

945 B.C. AM 3030   **REHOBOAM** 2 CHR. 11; 2 CHR. 12   ABIJAM / ABIJAH   ASA   921 B.C. JEHOSHAPHAT BORN (1 KI. 22:42).   35th YR. (2 CHR. 20:31)   896 B.C. JEHORAM 32 YR. (2 KI. 8:17).

RULES OVER ALL JUDAH AND BENJAMIN (1 KI. 12:16-24). SEE (1 KI. 11:31; EZRA 1:5).   928 B.C. AM 3047   926 B.C. AM 3049   ABIJAH AND ASA WERE BROTHERS (1 KI. 15:2, 10)   ASA DISEASED IN HIS FEET. (2 CHR. 16:12-14)   887 B.C. AM 3088

(1 KI. 14:21, 31)   17 YR.   (2 CHR. 12:13)   1 KI. 15:2   3 YR.   (1 KI. 15:10)   41 YR.   (1 KI. 15:10). (2 CHR. 16:13)

941 B.C. AM 3034   SHISHAK OF EGYPT TAKES THE TREASURES OF SOLOMON'S TEMPLE AND HOUSE TO EGYPT (2 CHR. 12:2-9).

SALVATION WAS PROMISED TO ALL STRANGERS AMONG YOU. (EX. 12:19, 49; NUM. 9:14; NUM. 15:15-16; DEUT. 29:14-15; ESTHER 8:17).

JEROBOAM BEGAN HIS REIGN OVER ISRAEL, WITH IDOL WORSHIP, USING GOLDEN CALVES. (1 KI. 12:25-33).

KINGS

889 B.C. AM 3086

FIRST

FIRST KINGS

GOD ANSWERS ELIJAH BY FIRE (1 KI. 18).

JOEL   DURING THE FAMINE OF AHAB

888 TO 885 B.C.   JOEL

985 B.C. TO 539 B.C. 2 CHR. 36:22   THE SECOND BOOK OF CHRONICLES

The last year of a king's reign was also counted as the first year of his successor's reign. Therefore there was a build-up of one unexpired year with each succession.

Total length of Israel's 18 king's reigns	242 years
Subtract the 18 unexpired build-up years	18 years
Expired years from 945 B.C. to 721 B.C.	224 years

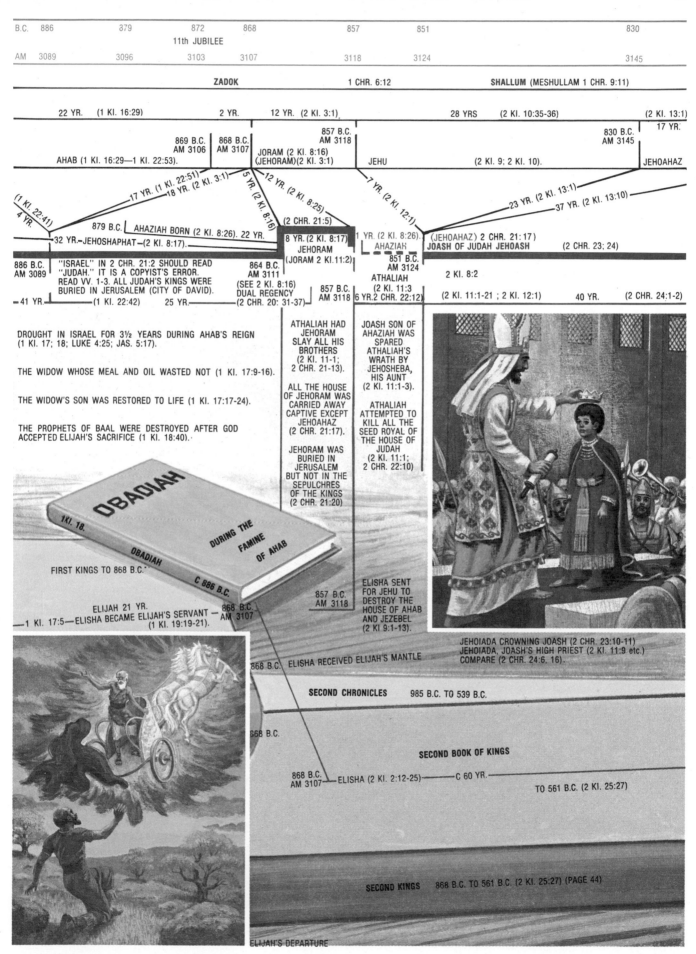

B.C.	886	879	872	868	857	851		830
			11th JUBILEE					
AM	3089	3096	3103	3107	3118	3124		3145

ZADOK   1 CHR. 6:12   SHALLUM (MESHULLAM 1 CHR. 9:11)

22 YR. (1 KI. 16:29)   2 YR.   12 YR. (2 KI. 3:1)   28 YRS (2 KI. 10:35-36)   (2 KI. 13:1)

857 B.C.
AM 3118
17 YR.

869 B.C.   868 B.C.
AM 3106   AM 3107

830 B.C.
AM 3145

JORAM (2 KI. 8:16)
(JEHORAM)(2 KI. 3:1)

AHAB (1 KI. 16:29—1 KI. 22:53).   JEHU   (2 KI. 9; 2 KI. 10).   JEHOAHAZ

17 YR. (1 KI. 22:51)
18 YR. (2 KI. 3:1)
5 YR. (2 KI. 8:16)
12 YR. (2 KI. 8:25)
7 YR. (2 KI. 12:1)
23 YR. (2 KI. 13:1)
37 YR. (2 KI. 13:10)

(1 KI. 22:41)
4 YR.

879 B.C.   AHAZIAH BORN (2 KI. 8:26). 22 YR.   (2 CHR. 21:5)
1 YR. (2 KI. 8:26)
(JEHOAHAZ) 2 CHR. 21:17)

32 YR.-JEHOSHAPHAT-(2 KI. 8:17).   8 YR. (2 KI. 8:17)   AHAZIAH   JOASH OF JUDAH JEHOASH   (2 CHR. 23; 24)

JEHORAM
(JORAM 2 KI.11:2)

886 B.C.
AM 3089

"ISRAEL" IN 2 CHR. 21:2 SHOULD READ
"JUDAH." IT IS A COPYIST'S ERROR.
READ VV. 1-3. ALL JUDAH'S KINGS WERE
BURIED IN JERUSALEM (CITY OF DAVID).

864 B.C.
AM 3111

851 B.C.
AM 3124

ATHALIAH
(2 KI. 11:3
6 YR. 2 CHR. 22:12)

2 KI. 8:2

(SEE 2 KI. 8:16)
DUAL REGENCY
(2 CHR. 20: 31-37)

857 B.C.
AM 3118

(2 KI. 11:1-21 ; 2 KI. 12:1)   40 YR.   (2 CHR. 24:1-2)

41 YR.   (1 KI. 22:42)   25 YR.

DROUGHT IN ISRAEL FOR 3½ YEARS DURING AHAB'S REIGN
(1 KI. 17; 18; LUKE 4:25; JAS. 5:17).

THE WIDOW WHOSE MEAL AND OIL WASTED NOT (1 KI. 17:9-16).

THE WIDOW'S SON WAS RESTORED TO LIFE (1 KI. 17:17-24).

THE PROPHETS OF BAAL WERE DESTROYED AFTER GOD
ACCEPTED ELIJAH'S SACRIFICE (1 KI. 18:40).

ATHALIAH HAD
JEHORAM
SLAY ALL HIS
BROTHERS
(2 KI. 11-1;
2 CHR. 21-13).

ALL THE HOUSE
OF JEHORAM WAS
CARRIED AWAY
CAPTIVE EXCEPT
JEHOAHAZ
(2 CHR. 21:17).

JEHORAM WAS
BURIED IN
JERUSALEM
BUT NOT IN THE
SEPULCHRES
OF THE KINGS
(2 CHR. 21:20)

JOASH SON OF
AHAZIAH WAS
SPARED
ATHALIAH'S
WRATH BY
JEHOSHEBA,
HIS AUNT
(2 KI. 11:1-3).

ATHALIAH
ATTEMPTED TO
KILL ALL THE
SEED ROYAL OF
THE HOUSE OF
JUDAH
(2 KI. 11:1;
2 CHR. 22:10)

OBADIAH

1 KI. 18.

OBADIAH

DURING THE
FAMINE
OF AHAB

FIRST KINGS TO 868 B.C.

C 886 B.C.

ELIJAH 21 YR.

1 KI. 17:5—ELISHA BECAME ELIJAH'S SERVANT
(1 KI. 19:19-21).

868 B.C.
AM 3107

857 B.C.
AM 3118

ELISHA SENT
FOR JEHU TO
DESTROY THE
HOUSE OF AHAB
AND JEZEBEL
(2 KI. 9:1-13).

JEHOIADA CROWNING JOASH (2 CHR. 23:10-11)
JEHOIADA, JOASH'S HIGH PRIEST (2 KI. 11:9 etc.)
COMPARE (2 CHR. 24:6, 16).

868 B.C. ELISHA RECEIVED ELIJAH'S MANTLE

SECOND CHRONICLES   985 B.C. TO 539 B.C.

868 B.C.

SECOND BOOK OF KINGS

868 B.C.
AM 3107   ELISHA (2 KI. 2:12-25)   C 60 YR.

TO 561 B.C. (2 KI. 25:27)

SECOND KINGS   868 B.C. TO 561 B.C. (2 KI. 25:27) (PAGE 44)

ELIJAH'S DEPARTURE

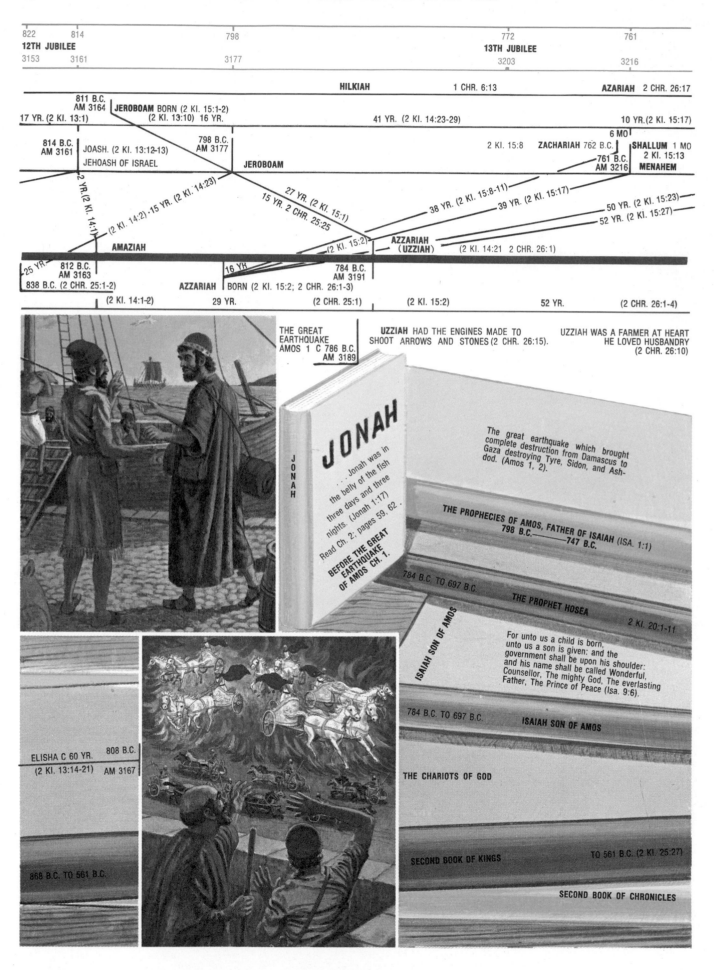

822   814   798   772   761
12TH JUBILEE   **13TH JUBILEE**
3153   3161   3177   3203   3216

HILKIAH   1 CHR. 6:13   **AZARIAH**   2 CHR. 26:17

811 B.C. AM 3164   **JEROBOAM** BORN (2 KI. 15:1-2)
17 YR. (2 KI. 13:1)   (2 KI. 13:10) 16 YR.   41 YR. (2 KI. 14:23-29)   10 YR.(2 KI. 15:17)

6 MO

814 B.C. AM 3161   JOASH. (2 KI. 13:12-13)   798 B.C. AM 3177   2 KI. 15:8   **ZACHARIAH** 762 B.C.   **SHALLUM** 1 MO 2 KI. 15:13
JEHOASH OF ISRAEL   **JEROBOAM**   761 B.C. AM 3216   **MENAHEM**

2 YR.(2 KI. 14:1)

27 YR. (2 KI. 15:1)   38 YR. (2 KI. 15:8-11)   39 YR. (2 KI. 15:17)
(2 KI. 14:2) 15 YR. (2 KI. 14:23)   15 YR. 2 CHR. 25:25   50 YR. (2 KI. 15:23)
52 YR. (2 KI. 15:27)

AMAZIAH   (2 KI. 15:2)   **AZARIAH**   (2 KI. 14:21 2 CHR. 26:1)
    (UZZIAH)

25 YR   812 B.C. AM 3163   16 YR   784 B.C. AM 3191
838 B.C. (2 CHR. 25:1-2)   **AZARIAH** BORN (2 KI. 15:2; 2 CHR. 26:1-3)

(2 KI. 14:1-2)   29 YR.   (2 CHR. 25:1)   (2 KI. 15:2)   52 YR.   (2 CHR. 26:1-4)

THE GREAT EARTHQUAKE AMOS 1 C 786 B.C. AM 3189

UZZIAH HAD THE ENGINES MADE TO SHOOT ARROWS AND STONES (2 CHR. 26:15).

UZZIAH WAS A FARMER AT HEART HE LOVED HUSBANDRY (2 CHR. 26:10)

JONAH

... Jonah was in the belly of the fish three days and three nights. (Jonah 1:17)

Read Ch. 2; pages 59, 62.

BEFORE THE GREAT EARTHQUAKE OF AMOS CH. 1.

The great earthquake which brought complete destruction from Damascus to Gaza destroying Tyre, Sidon, and Ashdod. (Amos 1, 2).

THE PROPHECIES OF AMOS, FATHER OF ISAIAH (ISA. 1:1) 798 B.C.——747 B.C.

784 B.C. TO 697 B.C.   **THE PROPHET HOSEA**   2 KI. 20:1-11

ISAIAH SON OF AMOS

For unto us a child is born, unto us a son is given: and the government shall be upon his shoulder: and his name shall be called Wonderful, Counsellor, The mighty God, The everlasting Father, The Prince of Peace (Isa. 9:6).

784 B.C. TO 697 B.C.   **ISAIAH SON OF AMOS**

ELISHA C 60 YR.   808 B.C. (2 KI. 13:14-21)   AM 3167

THE CHARIOTS OF GOD

868 B.C. TO 561 B.C.

SECOND BOOK OF KINGS   TO 561 B.C. (2 KI. 25:27)

SECOND BOOK OF CHRONICLES

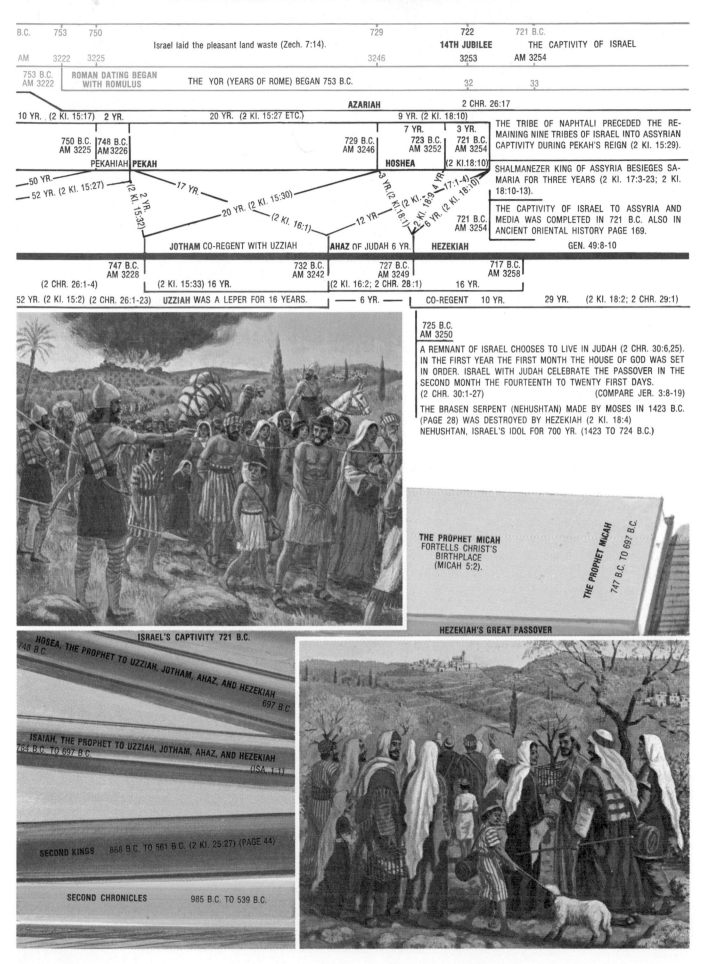

B.C.	753	750			729	**722**	721 B.C.
			Israel laid the pleasant land waste (Zech. 7:14).			**14TH JUBILEE**	THE CAPTIVITY OF ISRAEL
AM	3222	3225			3246	3253	AM 3254

753 B.C.
AM 3222   ROMAN DATING BEGAN WITH ROMULUS   THE YOR (YEARS OF ROME) BEGAN 753 B.C.   32   33

AZARIAH   2 CHR. 26:17

10 YR. (2 KI. 15:17) 2 YR.   20 YR. (2 KI. 15:27 ETC.)   9 YR. (2 KI. 18:10)

7 YR.   3 YR.

THE TRIBE OF NAPHTALI PRECEDED THE REMAINING NINE TRIBES OF ISRAEL INTO ASSYRIAN CAPTIVITY DURING PEKAH'S REIGN (2 KI. 15:29).

750 B.C. 748 B.C.   729 B.C.   723 B.C.   721 B.C.
AM 3225 AM 3226   AM 3246   AM 3252   AM 3254

PEKAHIAH **PEKAH**   **HOSHEA**   (2 KI.18:10)

SHALMANEZER KING OF ASSYRIA BESIEGES SAMARIA FOR THREE YEARS (2 KI. 17:3-23; 2 KI. 18:10-13).

50 YR.
52 YR. (2 KI. 15:27)   (2 KI. 15:32) 17 YR.   3 YR.(2 KI. 15:30)   (17:1-4)

THE CAPTIVITY OF ISRAEL TO ASSYRIA AND MEDIA WAS COMPLETED IN 721 B.C. ALSO IN ANCIENT ORIENTAL HISTORY PAGE 169.

2 YR. (2 KI. 15:32)   20 YR. (2 KI. 15:30)   (2 KI. 16:1)   12 YR. (2 KI.18:1)   2 YR. (2 KI. 18:9) 6 YR. (2 KI. 18:10)   721 B.C.
AM 3254

GEN. 49:8-10

JOTHAM CO-REGENT WITH UZZIAH   **AHAZ** OF JUDAH 6 YR.   **HEZEKIAH**

747 B.C.   732 B.C.   727 B.C.   717 B.C.
AM 3228   AM 3242   AM 3249   AM 3258

(2 CHR. 26:1-4)   (2 KI. 15:33) 16 YR.   (2 KI. 16:2; 2 CHR. 28:1) 16 YR.

52 YR. (2 KI. 15:2) (2 CHR. 26:1-23) **UZZIAH** WAS A LEPER FOR 16 YEARS.   — 6 YR. —   CO-REGENT 10 YR.   29 YR.   (2 KI. 18:2; 2 CHR. 29:1)

725 B.C.
AM 3250

A REMNANT OF ISRAEL CHOOSES TO LIVE IN JUDAH (2 CHR. 30:6,25). IN THE FIRST YEAR THE FIRST MONTH THE HOUSE OF GOD WAS SET IN ORDER. ISRAEL WITH JUDAH CELEBRATE THE PASSOVER IN THE SECOND MONTH THE FOURTEENTH TO TWENTY FIRST DAYS.
(2 CHR. 30:1-27)   (COMPARE JER. 3:8-19)

THE BRASEN SERPENT (NEHUSHTAN) MADE BY MOSES IN 1423 B.C. (PAGE 28) WAS DESTROYED BY HEZEKIAH (2 KI. 18:4) NEHUSHTAN, ISRAEL'S IDOL FOR 700 YR. (1423 TO 724 B.C.)

THE PROPHET MICAH
FORTELLS CHRIST'S BIRTHPLACE
(MICAH 5:2).

THE PROPHET MICAH
747 B.C. TO 697 B.C.

HEZEKIAH'S GREAT PASSOVER

ISRAEL'S CAPTIVITY 721 B.C.

HOSEA, THE PROPHET TO UZZIAH, JOTHAM, AHAZ, AND HEZEKIAH
748 B.C.   697 B.C.

ISAIAH, THE PROPHET TO UZZIAH, JOTHAM, AHAZ, AND HEZEKIAH
784 B.C. TO 697 B.C.   (ISA. 1:1)

SECOND KINGS   868 B.C. TO 561 B.C. (2 KI. 25:27) (PAGE 44)

SECOND CHRONICLES   985 B.C. TO 539 B.C.

B.C. 712	697	672 15th JUBILEE	622 16th JUBILEE
AM 3263	3278	3303	3353
YOR		82	132

SERAIAH 2 KI. 25:18   1 CHR. 6:14   JEHOZADAK 1 CHR. 6:15

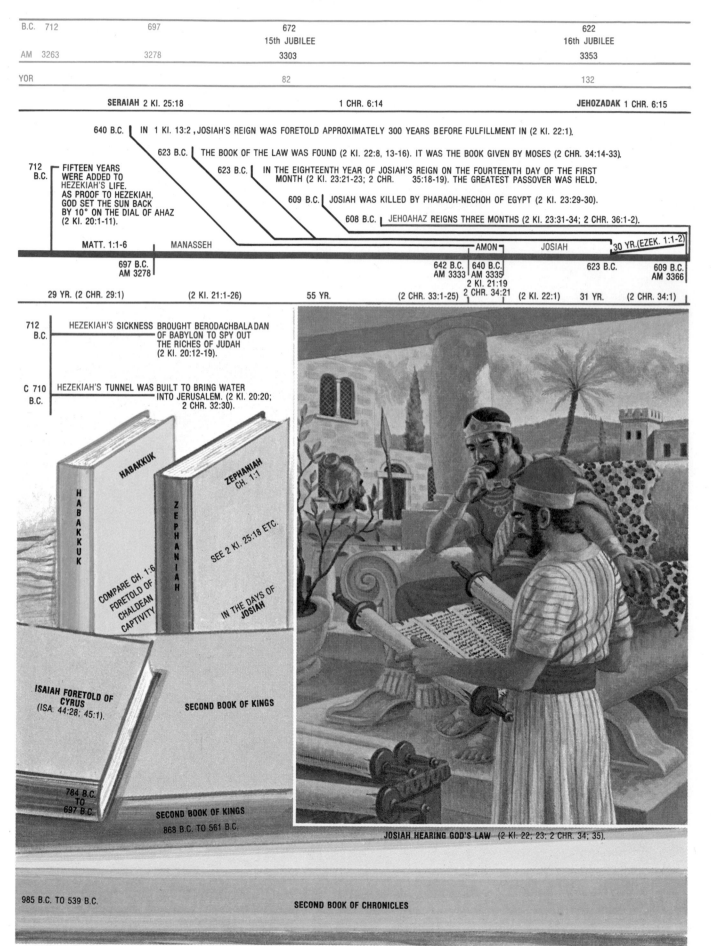

640 B.C.   IN 1 KI. 13:2, JOSIAH'S REIGN WAS FORETOLD APPROXIMATELY 300 YEARS BEFORE FULFILLMENT IN (2 KI. 22:1).

623 B.C.   THE BOOK OF THE LAW WAS FOUND (2 KI. 22:8, 13-16). IT WAS THE BOOK GIVEN BY MOSES (2 CHR. 34:14-33).

623 B.C.   IN THE EIGHTEENTH YEAR OF JOSIAH'S REIGN ON THE FOURTEENTH DAY OF THE FIRST MONTH (2 KI. 23:21-23; 2 CHR. 35:18-19). THE GREATEST PASSOVER WAS HELD.

609 B.C.   JOSIAH WAS KILLED BY PHARAOH-NECHOH OF EGYPT (2 KI. 23:29-30).

608 B.C.   JEHOAHAZ REIGNS THREE MONTHS (2 KI. 23:31-34; 2 CHR. 36:1-2).

712 B.C.   FIFTEEN YEARS WERE ADDED TO HEZEKIAH'S LIFE. AS PROOF TO HEZEKIAH, GOD SET THE SUN BACK BY 10° ON THE DIAL OF AHAZ (2 KI. 20:1-11).

MATT. 1:1-6   MANASSEH   AMON   JOSIAH   30 YR.(EZEK. 1:1-2)

697 B.C. AM 3278	642 B.C. AM 3333	640 B.C. AM 3335 2 KI. 21:19	623 B.C.	609 B.C. AM 3366
29 YR. (2 CHR. 29:1)	(2 KI. 21:1-26)	55 YR.	(2 CHR. 33:1-25)	2 CHR. 34:21 (2 KI. 22:1)	31 YR.	(2 CHR. 34:1)

712 B.C.   HEZEKIAH'S SICKNESS BROUGHT BERODACHBALADAN OF BABYLON TO SPY OUT THE RICHES OF JUDAH (2 KI. 20:12-19).

C 710 B.C.   HEZEKIAH'S TUNNEL WAS BUILT TO BRING WATER INTO JERUSALEM. (2 KI. 20:20; 2 CHR. 32:30).

HABAKKUK

HABAKKUK COMPARE CH. 1:6 FORETOLD OF CHALDEAN CAPTIVITY

ZEPHANIAH CH. 1:1

ZEPHANIAH SEE 2 KI. 25:18 ETC. IN THE DAYS OF JOSIAH

ISAIAH FORETOLD OF CYRUS (ISA. 44:28; 45:1).

SECOND BOOK OF KINGS

784 B.C. TO 697 B.C.

SECOND BOOK OF KINGS 868 B.C. TO 561 B.C.

JOSIAH HEARING GOD'S LAW (2 KI. 22; 23; 2 CHR. 34; 35).

985 B.C. TO 539 B.C.   SECOND BOOK OF CHRONICLES

B.C.	608	605	597	586	572 17th JUBILEE
AM	3367	3370	3378	3389	3403
YOR		149			182

JEHOZADAK (1 CHR. 6:15).

JOIADA

605 B.C. **NEBUCHADNEZZAR** AM 3370 (**NEBUCHADREZZAR**)

Judah with Benjamin and their portion of the Levites, are the two tribes in Babylonian captivity (Ezra 1:5; Ezra 4:1; Ezra 10:9; (Esther 2:5; 2 KI. 25:8-21).

587 B.C. AM 3388 18 YR. OF NEBUCHADNEZZAR (JER. 32:1)

(2 KI. 25:8) C 580 B.C. AM 3395 NEBUZ ARADAN CO-REGENT

19 YR. OF NEBUCHADREZZAR (JER. 52:12)

593 B.C. AM 3382 EZEKIEL BEGAN HIS PROPHECIES 5 YR. OF JEHOIACHIN

4 YR. (JER. 25:1)

19 YR. (2 KI. 25:8;

8 YR. (2 KI. 24:12, 8-16)

(JER. 32:1) 10 YR.

JER. 52:12)

37 YR. (2 KI. 25:27-30; JER. 52:31)

30 YR. EZEK. 1:1,2

598 B.C.

JEHOIACHIN 3 MOS. (**MATTANIAH** (2 KI. 24:17) **ZEDEKIAH**)(2 KI. 24:18-20; JER. 52:1)

JECONIAH (1 CHR. 3:16) **JECHONIAS** (MATT. 1:11)

TRIBUTE 2 KI. 23:33

ELIAKIM (**JEHOIAKIM**) (2 CHR. 36:4)

GEN. 49:8-10

608 B.C. AM 3367

597 B.C. AM 3378

586 B.C. AM 3389

CARRYING AWAY INTO BABYLON (2 KI. 25:8-21; JER. 25:11) 70 YEARS OF CAPTIVITY. COMPLETED 516 B.C. (PAGE 45).

(2 KI. 23:34—24:7; 2 CHR. 36:5) 11 YR.

(2 KI. 24:18—25:7). 11 YR. (2 CHR. 36:11)

C 604 B.C. SHADRACH, MESHECH, ABEDNEGO, AND DANIEL WERE BROUGHT TO BABYLON FOR SCHOOLING (DAN. 1:1-20).

NEBUCHADNEZZAR'S DREAM OF HIS IMAGE IN GOLD. NINETY FEET HIGH, 9 FEET WIDE. (DAN. 2; 3:1-7).

SHADRACH, MESHECH, AND ABEDNEGO WERE CAST INTO THE FURNACE HEATED 1/7th HOTTER THAN NORMAL (DAN. 3:8-30).

NEBUCHADNEZZAR'S DREAM OF THE TREE, AND THE INTERPRETATION BY DANIEL (DAN. 4:1-28).

C 597 B.C. NEBUCHADNEZZAR BESIEGES JERUSALEM (JER. 52:1-5).

595 B.C. NEBUCHADNEZZAR BEHAVED AS AN ANIMAL FOR SEVEN YEARS (DAN. 4:28-33).

588 B.C. NEBUCHADNEZZAR, THE CONVERTED MAN (DAN. 4:34-37).

586 B.C. NEBUZZARADAN AM 3389 COMPLETES THE CARRYING AWAY INTO BABYLON (2 KI. 25:8-21; JER. 52:12-34).

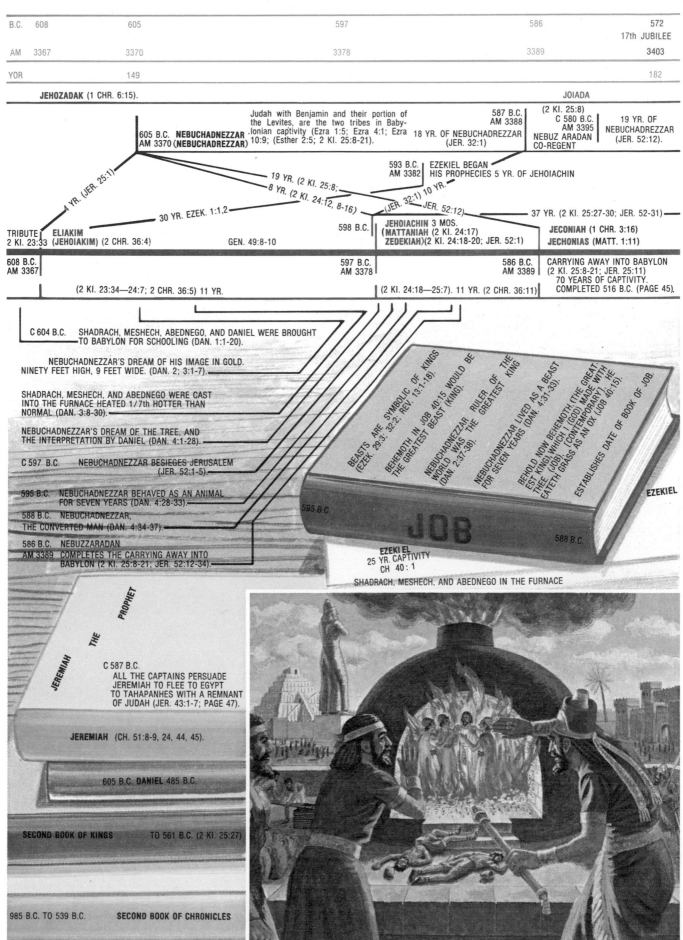

BEASTS ARE SYMBOLIC OF KINGS (EZEK. 29:3; 32:2; REV. 13:1-18).

BEHEMOTH IN JOB 40:15 WOULD BE THE GREATEST BEAST (KING).

NEBUCHADNEZZAR RULER OF THE WORLD WAS THE GREATEST KING (DAN. 2:37-38).

NEBUCHADNEZZAR LIVED AS A BEAST FOR SEVEN YEARS (DAN. 4:31-33).

BEHOLD NOW BEHEMOTH (THE GREATEST KING) WHICH I (GOD) MADE WITH THEE (JOB), (CONTEMPORARY) HE EATETH GRASS AS AN OX (JOB 40:15).

ESTABLISHES DATE OF BOOK OF JOB.

EZEKIEL

595 B.C.

JOB

588 B.C.

EZEKIEL 25 YR. CAPTIVITY CH 40:1

SHADRACH, MESHECH, AND ABEDNEGO IN THE FURNACE

JEREMIAH THE PROPHET

C 587 B.C. ALL THE CAPTAINS PERSUADE JEREMIAH TO FLEE TO EGYPT TO TAHAPANHES WITH A REMNANT OF JUDAH (JER. 43:1-7; PAGE 47).

JEREMIAH (CH. 51:8-9, 24, 44, 45).

605 B.C. **DANIEL** 485 B.C.

SECOND BOOK OF KINGS TO 561 B.C. (2 KI. 25:27)

985 B.C. TO 539 B.C. **SECOND BOOK OF CHRONICLES**

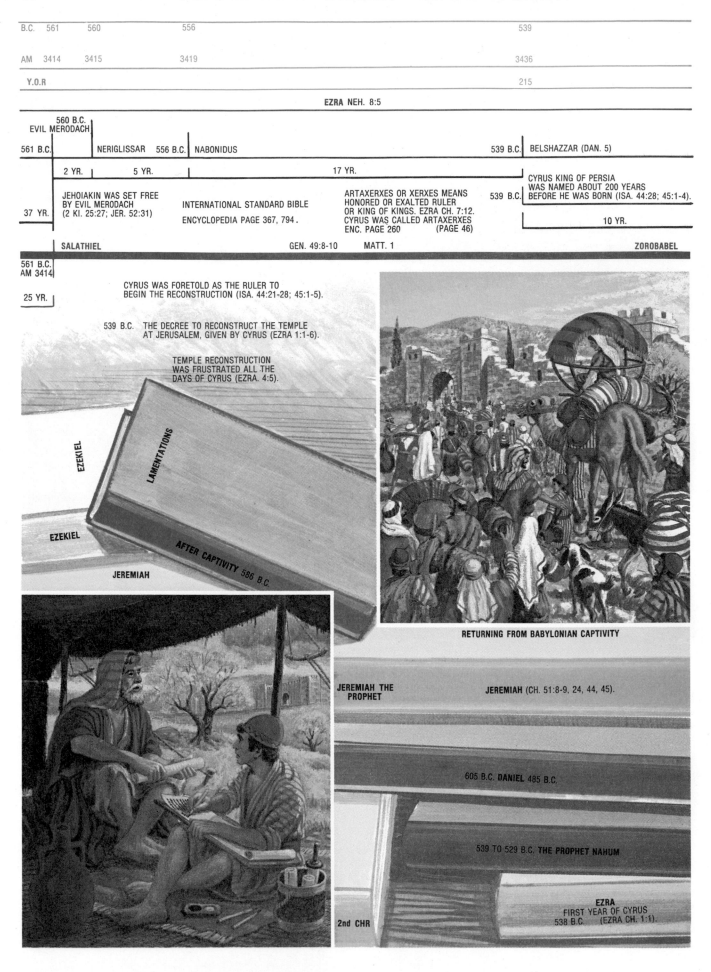

B.C.	561	560	556		539
AM	3414	3415	3419		3436
Y.O.R					215

EZRA NEH. 8:5

560 B.C.
EVIL MERODACH

561 B.C. — NERIGLISSAR — 556 B.C. NABONIDUS — 539 B.C. BELSHAZZAR (DAN. 5)

2 YR. | 5 YR. | 17 YR.

CYRUS KING OF PERSIA
WAS NAMED ABOUT 200 YEARS
539 B.C. BEFORE HE WAS BORN (ISA. 44:28; 45:1-4).

37 YR.

JEHOIAKIN WAS SET FREE
BY EVIL MERODACH
(2 KI. 25:27; JER. 52:31)

INTERNATIONAL STANDARD BIBLE
ENCYCLOPEDIA PAGE 367, 794.

ARTAXERXES OR XERXES MEANS
HONORED OR EXALTED RULER
OR KING OF KINGS. EZRA CH. 7:12.
CYRUS WAS CALLED ARTAXERXES
ENC. PAGE 260   (PAGE 46)

10 YR.

SALATHIEL   GEN. 49:8-10   MATT. 1   ZOROBABEL

561 B.C.
AM 3414

25 YR.

CYRUS WAS FORETOLD AS THE RULER TO
BEGIN THE RECONSTRUCTION (ISA. 44:21-28; 45:1-5).

539 B.C.   THE DECREE TO RECONSTRUCT THE TEMPLE
AT JERUSALEM, GIVEN BY CYRUS (EZRA 1:1-6).

TEMPLE RECONSTRUCTION
WAS FRUSTRATED ALL THE
DAYS OF CYRUS (EZRA. 4:5).

EZEKIEL

LAMENTATIONS

EZEKIEL

AFTER CAPTIVITY 586 B.C.

JEREMIAH

RETURNING FROM BABYLONIAN CAPTIVITY

JEREMIAH THE
PROPHET

JEREMIAH (CH. 51:8-9, 24, 44, 45).

605 B.C. DANIEL 485 B.C.

539 TO 529 B.C. THE PROPHET NAHUM

2nd CHR

EZRA
FIRST YEAR OF CYRUS
538 B.C.   (EZRA CH. 1:1).

B.C.	529	522	516
		18th JUBILEE	
AM	3446	3453	3459
		232	

EZRA NEH. 8:5

| INTERNATIONAL STANDARD BIBLE ENCYCLOPEDIA PAGE 367, 368 | 522 B.C. AM 3453 | DARIUS, (ARTAXERXES OF PERSIA) 62 YEARS OLD (EZRA 6:14-15; DAN. 5:31) | 516 B.C. AM 3459 |

| SAME PERSON | CAMBYSES (AHASUERUS) IN (EZRA 4:6) (ARTAXERXES KING OF PERSIA) IN (EZRA 4:7) | 522 B.C. | DARIUS ORDERS THE RECORDS OF CYRUS SEARCHED, AND COMMANDS THE TEMPLE RECONSTRUCTION TO CONTINUE. COMPLETED IN THE TWELFTH MONTH, IN THE SIXTH YEAR OF HIS REIGN (EZRA 6:1-15). |

529 B.C.   AHASUERUS (EZRA 4:6) (CAMBYSES)

THE REBUILT TEMPLE

UNDER ZOROBABEL WAS COMPLETED (EZRA 6:15; ZECH. 4:9)

| 10 YR. | (SEE PAGE 44) | 7 YR. | CAMBYSES DECREED TO STOP THE REBUILDING OF THE TEMPLE (EZRA 4:4-24) |

70 YEARS COMPLETED (DAN. 9:1-2; ZECH. 7:5)

ZOROBABEL   (MATT. 1)

TEMPLE DIMENSIONS (1 KI. 6:7; 1 CHR. 3:3-4)

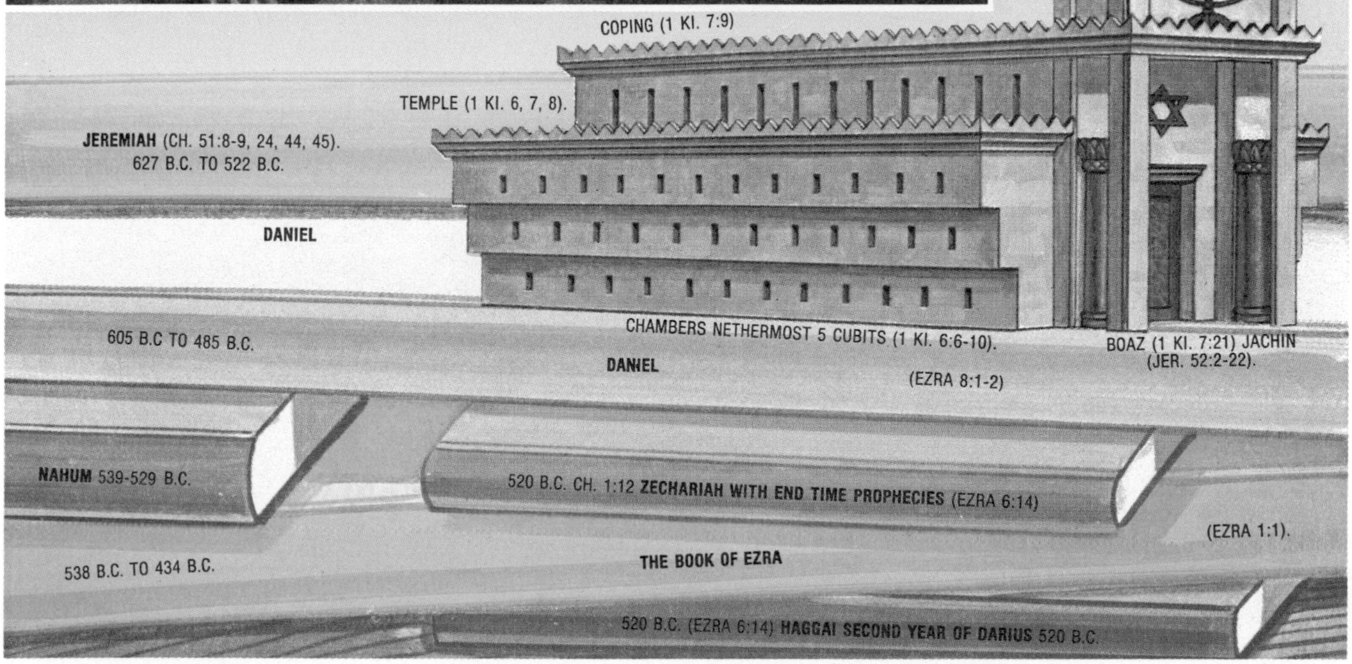

COPING (1 KI. 7:9)

TEMPLE (1 KI. 6, 7, 8).

JEREMIAH (CH. 51:8-9, 24, 44, 45). 627 B.C. TO 522 B.C.

DANIEL

HOLINESS UNTO THE LORD

605 B.C TO 485 B.C.

CHAMBERS NETHERMOST 5 CUBITS (1 KI. 6:6-10).

DANIEL   (EZRA 8:1-2)

BOAZ (1 KI. 7:21) JACHIN (JER. 52:2-22).

NAHUM 539-529 B.C.

520 B.C. CH. 1:12 ZECHARIAH WITH END TIME PROPHECIES (EZRA 6:14)

(EZRA 1:1).

538 B.C. TO 434 B.C.   THE BOOK OF EZRA

520 B.C. (EZRA 6:14) HAGGAI SECOND YEAR OF DARIUS 520 B.C.

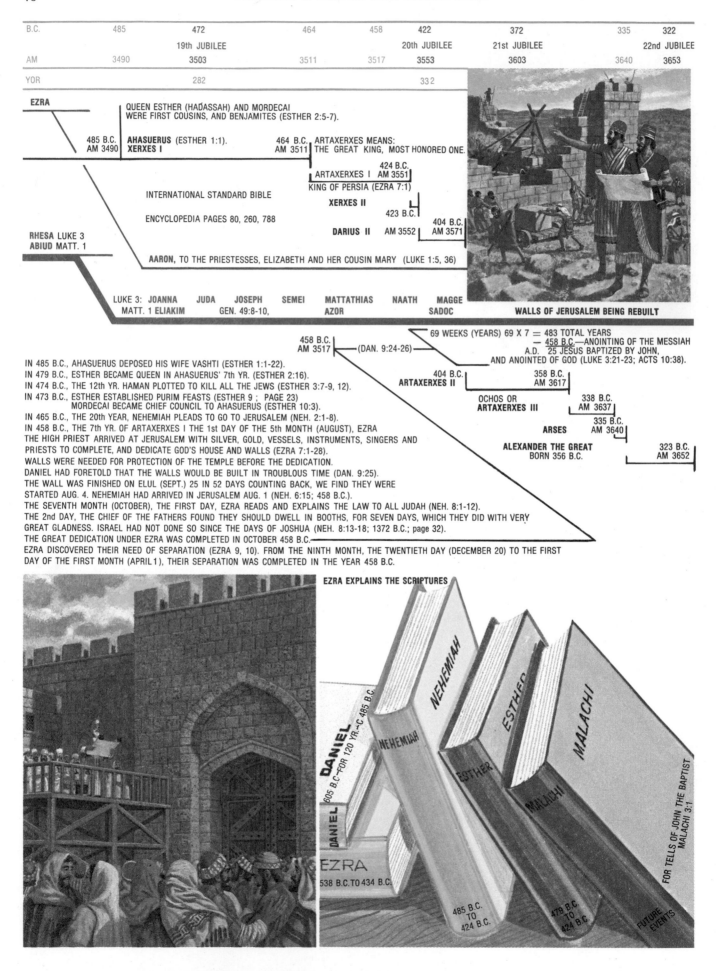

B.C.	485	472	464	458	422	372	335	322
		19th JUBILEE			20th JUBILEE	21st JUBILEE		22nd JUBILEE
AM	3490	3503	3511	3517	3553	3603	3640	3653
YOR		282			332			

EZRA

QUEEN ESTHER (HADASSAH) AND MORDECAI
WERE FIRST COUSINS, AND BENJAMITES (ESTHER 2:5-7).

485 B.C.   **AHASUERUS** (ESTHER 1:1).   464 B.C.   ARTAXERXES MEANS:
AM 3490   **XERXES I**   AM 3511   THE GREAT KING, MOST HONORED ONE.

424 B.C.
ARTAXERXES I   AM 3551
KING OF PERSIA (EZRA 7:1)

INTERNATIONAL STANDARD BIBLE

XERXES II

ENCYCLOPEDIA PAGES 80, 260, 788   423 B.C.   404 B.C.
DARIUS II   AM 3552   AM 3571

RHESA LUKE 3
ABIUD MATT. 1

AARON, TO THE PRIESTESSES, ELIZABETH AND HER COUSIN MARY (LUKE 1:5, 36)

LUKE 3: **JOANNA**   **JUDA**   **JOSEPH**   **SEMEI**   **MATTATHIAS**   **NAATH**   **MAGGE**
MATT. 1 **ELIAKIM**   GEN. 49:8-10,   **AZOR**   **SADOC**

WALLS OF JERUSALEM BEING REBUILT

69 WEEKS (YEARS) 69 X 7 = 483 TOTAL YEARS

458 B.C.   458 B.C.—ANOINTING OF THE MESSIAH
AM 3517   (DAN. 9:24-26)   A.D. 25 JESUS BAPTIZED BY JOHN,
AND ANOINTED OF GOD (LUKE 3:21-23; ACTS 10:38).

404 B.C.   358 B.C.
ARTAXERXES II   AM 3617

OCHOS OR   338 B.C.
ARTAXERXES III   AM 3637

335 B.C.
ARSES   AM 3640

ALEXANDER THE GREAT   323 B.C.
BORN 356 B.C.   AM 3652

IN 485 B.C., AHASUERUS DEPOSED HIS WIFE VASHTI (ESTHER 1:1-22).
IN 479 B.C., ESTHER BECAME QUEEN IN AHASUERUS' 7th YR. (ESTHER 2:16).
IN 474 B.C., THE 12th YR. HAMAN PLOTTED TO KILL ALL THE JEWS (ESTHER 3:7-9, 12).
IN 473 B.C., ESTHER ESTABLISHED PURIM FEASTS (ESTHER 9 ; PAGE 23)
MORDECAI BECAME CHIEF COUNCIL TO AHASUERUS (ESTHER 10:3).
IN 465 B.C., THE 20th YEAR, NEHEMIAH PLEADS TO GO TO JERUSALEM (NEH. 2:1-8).
IN 458 B.C., THE 7th YR. OF ARTAXERXES I THE 1st DAY OF THE 5th MONTH (AUGUST), EZRA
THE HIGH PRIEST ARRIVED AT JERUSALEM WITH SILVER, GOLD, VESSELS, INSTRUMENTS, SINGERS AND
PRIESTS TO COMPLETE, AND DEDICATE GOD'S HOUSE AND WALLS (EZRA 7:1-28).
WALLS WERE NEEDED FOR PROTECTION OF THE TEMPLE BEFORE THE DEDICATION.
DANIEL HAD FORETOLD THAT THE WALLS WOULD BE BUILT IN TROUBLOUS TIME (DAN. 9:25).
THE WALL WAS FINISHED ON ELUL (SEPT.) 25 IN 52 DAYS COUNTING BACK, WE FIND THEY WERE
STARTED AUG. 4. NEHEMIAH HAD ARRIVED IN JERUSALEM AUG. 1 (NEH. 6:15; 458 B.C.).
THE SEVENTH MONTH (OCTOBER), THE FIRST DAY, EZRA READS AND EXPLAINS THE LAW TO ALL JUDAH (NEH. 8:1-12).
THE 2nd DAY, THE CHIEF OF THE FATHERS FOUND THEY SHOULD DWELL IN BOOTHS, FOR SEVEN DAYS, WHICH THEY DID WITH VERY
GREAT GLADNESS. ISRAEL HAD NOT DONE SO SINCE THE DAYS OF JOSHUA (NEH. 8:13-18; 1372 B.C.; page 32).
THE GREAT DEDICATION UNDER EZRA WAS COMPLETED IN OCTOBER 458 B.C.
EZRA DISCOVERED THEIR NEED OF SEPARATION (EZRA 9, 10). FROM THE NINTH MONTH, THE TWENTIETH DAY (DECEMBER 20) TO THE FIRST
DAY OF THE FIRST MONTH (APRIL 1), THEIR SEPARATION WAS COMPLETED IN THE YEAR 458 B.C.

EZRA EXPLAINS THE SCRIPTURES

DANIEL 605 B.C.—FOR 120 YR.—C 485 B.C.

NEHEMIAH

ESTHER

MALACHI

EZRA 538 B.C. TO 434 B.C.

FOR TELLS OF JOHN THE BAPTIST MALACHI 3:1

485 B.C. TO 424 B.C.

479 B.C. TO 424 B.C.

FUTURE EVENTS

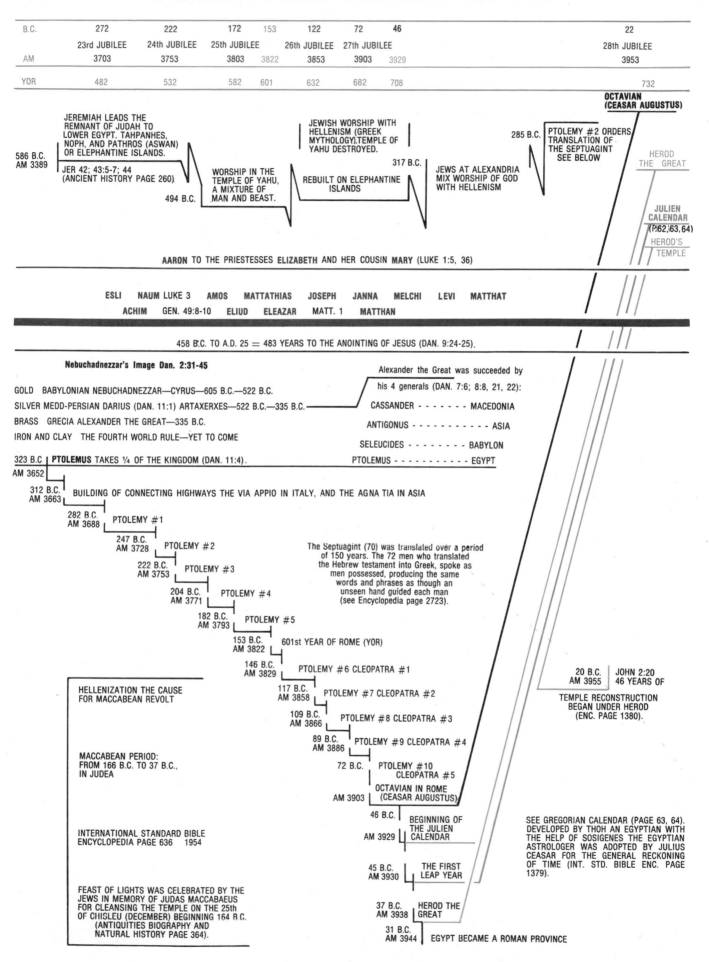

B.C.	272	222	172	153	122	72	46	22
	23rd JUBILEE	24th JUBILEE	25th JUBILEE		26th JUBILEE	27th JUBILEE		28th JUBILEE
AM	3703	3753	3803	3822	3853	3903	3929	3953
YOR	482	532	582	601	632	682	708	732

OCTAVIAN (CEASAR AUGUSTUS)

JEREMIAH LEADS THE REMNANT OF JUDAH TO LOWER EGYPT. TAHPANHES, NOPH, AND PATHROS (ASWAN) OR ELEPHANTINE ISLANDS.

586 B.C. AM 3389

JER 42; 43:5-7; 44 (ANCIENT HISTORY PAGE 260)

494 B.C.

WORSHIP IN THE TEMPLE OF YAHU, A MIXTURE OF MAN AND BEAST.

JEWISH WORSHIP WITH HELLENISM (GREEK MYTHOLOGY).TEMPLE OF YAHU DESTROYED.

REBUILT ON ELEPHANTINE ISLANDS

317 B.C.

JEWS AT ALEXANDRIA MIX WORSHIP OF GOD WITH HELLENISM

285 B.C. PTOLEMY #2 ORDERS TRANSLATION OF THE SEPTUAGINT SEE BELOW

HEROD THE GREAT

JULIEN CALENDAR (P. 62, 63, 64)

HEROD'S TEMPLE

AARON TO THE PRIESTESSES **ELIZABETH** AND HER COUSIN **MARY** (LUKE 1:5, 36)

ESLI	NAUM	LUKE 3	AMOS	MATTATHIAS	JOSEPH	JANNA	MELCHI	LEVI	MATTHAT
ACHIM		GEN. 49:8-10	ELIUD	ELEAZAR	MATT. 1	MATTHAN			

458 B.C. TO A.D. 25 = 483 YEARS TO THE ANOINTING OF JESUS (DAN. 9:24-25).

Nebuchadnezzar's Image Dan. 2:31-45

GOLD BABYLONIAN NEBUCHADNEZZAR—CYRUS—605 B.C.—522 B.C.

SILVER MEDD-PERSIAN DARIUS (DAN. 11:1) ARTAXERXES—522 B.C.—335 B.C.

BRASS GRECIA ALEXANDER THE GREAT—335 B.C.

IRON AND CLAY THE FOURTH WORLD RULE—YET TO COME

Alexander the Great was succeeded by his 4 generals (DAN. 7:6; 8:8, 21, 22):

CASSANDER	- - - - - -	MACEDONIA
ANTIGONUS	- - - - - - - - - -	ASIA
SELEUCIDES	- - - - - - -	BABYLON
PTOLEMUS	- - - - - - - - - -	EGYPT

323 B.C **PTOLEMUS** TAKES ¼ OF THE KINGDOM (DAN. 11:4).
AM 3652

312 B.C. BUILDING OF CONNECTING HIGHWAYS THE VIA APPIO IN ITALY, AND THE AGNA TIA IN ASIA
AM 3663

282 B.C. PTOLEMY #1
AM 3688

247 B.C. PTOLEMY #2
AM 3728

222 B.C. PTOLEMY #3
AM 3753

204 B.C. PTOLEMY #4
AM 3771

182 B.C. PTOLEMY #5
AM 3793

153 B.C. 601st YEAR OF ROME (YOR)
AM 3822

146 B.C. PTOLEMY #6 CLEOPATRA #1
AM 3829

117 B.C. PTOLEMY #7 CLEOPATRA #2
AM 3858

109 B.C. PTOLEMY #8 CLEOPATRA #3
AM 3866

89 B.C. PTOLEMY #9 CLEOPATRA #4
AM 3886

72 B.C. PTOLEMY #10 CLEOPATRA #5

OCTAVIAN IN ROME (CEASAR AUGUSTUS)
AM 3903

46 B.C. BEGINNING OF THE JULIEN CALENDAR
AM 3929

45 B.C. THE FIRST LEAP YEAR
AM 3930

37 B.C. HEROD THE GREAT
AM 3938

31 B.C. EGYPT BECAME A ROMAN PROVINCE
AM 3944

The Septuagint (70) was translated over a period of 150 years. The 72 men who translated the Hebrew testament into Greek, spoke as men possessed, producing the same words and phrases as though an unseen hand guided each man (see Encyclopedia page 2723).

HELLENIZATION THE CAUSE FOR MACCABEAN REVOLT

MACCABEAN PERIOD: FROM 166 B.C. TO 37 B.C., IN JUDEA

INTERNATIONAL STANDARD BIBLE ENCYCLOPEDIA PAGE 636 1954

FEAST OF LIGHTS WAS CELEBRATED BY THE JEWS IN MEMORY OF JUDAS MACCABAEUS FOR CLEANSING THE TEMPLE ON THE 25th OF CHISLEU (DECEMBER) BEGINNING 164 B.C. (ANTIQUITIES BIOGRAPHY AND NATURAL HISTORY PAGE 364).

20 B.C. JOHN 2:20
AM 3955 46 YEARS OF

TEMPLE RECONSTRUCTION BEGAN UNDER HEROD (ENC. PAGE 1380).

SEE GREGORIAN CALENDAR (PAGE 63, 64). DEVELOPED BY THOH AN EGYPTIAN WITH THE HELP OF SOSIGENES THE EGYPTIAN ASTROLOGER WAS ADOPTED BY JULIUS CEASAR FOR THE GENERAL RECKONING OF TIME (INT. STD. BIBLE ENC. PAGE 1379).

B.C.	17	13	9	7	TISHRI OCTOBER 7th MO.	JAN.	FEB.	MAR.	6 APR.	MAY	JUNE	JULY	AUGUST
AM 3954	3958	3962	3966	3968					3969				
YOR 733	737	741	745	747					748				

OCTAVIAN (CEASAR AUGUSTUS)

HOW MATTHEW'S AND LUKE'S GENEALOGIES OF CHRIST DIFFER

HEROD THE GREAT

From Abraham to David, their genealogies are identical. Then Luke follows the priestly lineage. The royal and priestly families intermarried several times. Their first merging was when Aaron, the first high priest, married into royalty. He married Elisheba, a daughter of Judah (Ex. 6:23). Elisheba's brother, Naashon, carried on the royal lineage (Matt. 1:4 ; page 19).

21 LEAP YEAR   17 LEAP YEAR

HEROD'S TEMPLE CONSTRUCTION

AARON TO ELIZABETH

Another example of the uniting of the two families occurred when David married Bathsheba, a priestess (see page 35). Luke's account lists several high priests. Lastly, Joseph, of Judah's family, married Mary of Aaron's family. Mary was a priestess as was her cousin Elizabeth (Luke 1:5,36).

HEROD THE GREAT

JULIEN CALENDAR

TEMPLE CONSTRUCTION
BEGAN 20 B.C

MARY (LUKE 1:5, 36)

HELI (LUKE 3:23)   JACOB (MATT. 1:16)   GEN. 49:8-10   JOSEPH, JESUS' FOSTER FATHER (MATT. 1:18; 24-25)

458 B.C. TO A.D. 25 = 483 YEARS TO THE ANOINTING OF JESUS (DAN. 9:24-25).

John the Baptist's father, Zacharias, was a high priest, because only a high priest could burn incense (Ex. 30:7). He held the high priest's office (Ex. 30:30; 40:13; Num. 18:7; Deut. 10:6). The high priest must go alone once a year into the holiest of all with blood for the atonement of all the people. That day was Oct. 10, the day of atonement, when the whole multitude of people were praying without at the time of incense (Luke 1:10). Zecharias was alone when Gabriel appeared unto him. The people were waiting without to hear that their sins were forgiven (Luke 1:10).

The dove, symbolic of The Holy Spirit (Holy Ghost) (Luke 3:22)

THE HOLY GHOST SHALL COME UPON THEE,
AND THE POWER OF THE HIGHEST SHALL
OVERSHADOW THEE: THEREFORE ALSO
THAT HOLY THING WHICH SHALL BE
BORN OF THEE SHALL BE CALLED
THE SON OF GOD
(LUKE: 1:35)

6 B.C.
AM 3969
4th MO. JULY
LUKE 1:26-55
THE ANNUNCIATION

FOR NOT BELIEVING THE ANGEL, ZACHARIAS WAS
STRICKEN DUMB, UNTIL HIS SON WAS BORN AND
NAMED JOHN. (READ LUKE 1:5-23, 57-66 ETC.).

B.C.						5 B.C.		4 B.C.		3 B.C.
SEPTEMBER	OCT.	NOV.	DEC.	JAN.	FEB.	MAR.	APRIL	MARCH	APRIL	MARCH
AM						AM 3970		AM 3971		AM 3972
						YOR 749		YOR 750		YOR 751

OCTAVIAN   (CEASAR AUGUSTUS)

HEROD THE GREAT

Herod the Great died about, 13th of Adar (March) the 12th month 4 B.C. YOR 750. Enc. pages 1381, 1628)

HEROD
ARCHELAUS
LYSANIAS
PHILIP

LEAP YEAR   JULIEN CALENDAR

HEROD'S TEMPLE CONSTRUCTION BEGAN 20 B.C.

MARY

The star is symbolic of Christ.

JOSEPH

THE SHEPHERDS AND THE ANGELS

458 B.C. TO A.D. 25 = 483 YEARS TO THE ANOINTING OF JESUS (DAN. 9:25)

6 B.C.
6th MO.
AM 3969

JOHN WAS BORN THE PROPHET OF THE HIGHEST, TO PREPARE THE WAY FOR CHRIST (LUKE 1:76).

JESUS CHRIST, GOD'S SON, BORN APRIL 1, 5 B.C. (AM 3970)

JOSEPH JESUS' FOSTER FATHER ADOPTED HIM. THIS MADE JESUS THE LEGAL HEIR TO KING DAVID'S EARTHLY THRONE. ALL BELIEVERS RECEIVE THE SPIRIT OF ADOPTION TO BECOME CHILDREN OF GOD (ROM. 8:15-17; GAL. 4:1-7). [LIKEWISE BY ADOPTION, WE BECOME LEGAL HEIRS WITH CHRIST TO GOD'S HEAVENLY THRONE].

BUT THOU, BETHLEHEM EPHRATAH, THOUGH THOU BE LITTLE AMONG THE THOUSANDS OF JUDAH, YET OUT OF THEE SHALL BE COME FORTH UNTO ME THAT IS TO BE RULER IN ISRAEL; WHOSE GOINGS FORTH HAVE BEEN FROM OF OLD, FROM EVERLASTING (MICAH 5:2).

JESUS, THE LAMB OF GOD WAS BORN AT THE SEASON WHEN OTHER PASSOVER LAMBS WERE BORN (JOHN 1:29). "A MALE OF THE FIRST YEAR" (EX. 12:5), WAS BORN THE PREVIOUS APRIL.

Herod's Decree

Herod the Great died about the 13th of March (Adar) in 4 B.C., in the year of Rome 750. Jesus was more than one year old, but less than two years old, when Herod decreed that all the children two years and under in and near Bethlehem should be slain (see Matt. 2:16). Jesus was 23½ months old when Herod died. Herod gave the order for the children to be slain while he was still alive. The time from April 1, 5 B.C. to March 13, 4 B.C. was 23½ months.

Veil, the type of Jesus' body

The veil of the temple, and of the tabernacle, typified the flesh (body) of Jesus(Heb. 10:5,10,20). When Jesus died the veil was rent in twain (Matt. 27:51; Mark 15:38; Luke 23:45). The veil, a part of the tabernacle; was first reared up at Sinai on April 1, 1461 B.C. (see Ex. 40:17). Jesus was in the pillar of the cloud that covered the tent of the testimony on April 1, as soon as the tabernacle was reared up (Num. 9:15); (Ex. 13:21; 14:19; 40:34-36). This is one evidence that Jesus would be born on an April 1. (see pages 25, 62).

NAMING OF JOHN THE BAPTIST (LUKE 1:58-80).

JOHN THE BAPTIST WAS BEHEADED BY HEROD THE TETRARCH IN A.D. 27 (SEE HARMONY OF THE GOSPELS, PAGE 54).

JOHN, A SECOND COUSIN TO JESUS, LIVED 32 YEARS (LUKE 1:36).

THEN JOSEPH BEING RAISED FROM SLEEP DID AS THE ANGEL OF THE LORD HAD BIDDEN HIM, AND TOOK UNTO HIM HIS WIFE: AND KNEW HER NOT TILL SHE HAD BROUGHT FORTH HER FIRSTBORN SON: AND CALLED HIS NAME JESUS (MATT. 1:18-25).

B.C. 2	B.C. 1	A.D. 1	6	8	11	14	20	25	C 6th MO. SEPT.
	—12 MO. PERIOD—								
AM 3973	3974	3975	3980	3982	3985	3988	3994	3999	
YOR 752	753	754	759	761	764	767	773	778	

OCTAVIAN (CEASAR AUGUSTUS), DIED IN A.D. 14 (ENC. 646, 2979).

A.D. 14
AM 3988

A.D. 11 CO-REGENT
AM 3985 TIBERIUS CEASAR (LUKE 3:1). (INT. STD. BIBLE ENC. PAGES 1628, 1381).

HEROD ANTIPAS TETRARCH OF GALILEE (LUKE 3:1). (INT. STD. BIBLE ENC. PAGE 1381).

ARCHELAUS AD6 ENC. 645 | PILATE (LUKE 3:1; 28:5-15) (INT. STD. BIBLE ENC. PAGE 2396)

LYSANIAS TETRARCH OF ABILENE· (LUKE 3:1). (INT. STD. BIBLE ENC. PAGE 1943).

PHILIP TETRARCH OF ITUREA AND TRACHONITES   (INT. STD. BIBLE ENC. PAGE 645)

JULIEN LEAP YEAR CALENDAR
A.D. 4 BEGAN THE A.D. 4-YEAR EVEN-NUMBER CYCLE OF LEAP YEARS (PAGES 62-63).

HEROD'S
TEMPLE CONSTRUCTION FROM 20 B.C TO A.D. 26 = 46 YEARS IN BUILDING (JOHN 2:20).

A.D. 11   A.D. 25

IN THE 15th YEAR OF TIBERIUS CAESAR (LUKE 3:1)

11 12 13 14 15 16 17 18 19 20 21 22 23 24 25
15 YEARS

C 6th MO. SEPT.
458 B.C. TO A.D. 25 = 483 YEARS TO   A.D. 25
THE ANOINTING OF JESUS (DAN. 9:25; PAGE 63) AM 3999

For all the prophets, and the law prophesied until John, John the Baptist came in the spirit and power of Elias (MAL. 4:5-6; MATT. 11:13-14).

AD 8 | Jesus was now full twelve years of age, before the passover
AM 3982 | feast. Jesus remained behind, and for three days confounded
YOR 761 | the scholars (LUKE 2:40-52).

James
Joses
Simon and sisters
Judas

The brothers of Jesus
(MATT. 13:55-56; MARK 6:3; 15:40;
GAL. 1:19) (SEE PAGE 54).

In the 4000th year after creation, Jesus was anointed of God.

Jesus Himself began to be about thirty years of age when He was baptized by John, and anointed of God (Luke 3:21-23).

JESUS CONFOUNDING THE SCHOLARS
LUKE 2:40-52

THE APOSTLES (DISCIPLES) OF JESUS
(Matt. 10:2-4; Mark 3:16-19; Luke 6:13-16)
THREE SETS OF BROTHERS AMONG THE TWELVE.

Andrew, brother of Peter

Peter, writer of books of Peter. Called Simon, or Cephas (a stone) (Matt. 16:18; John 1:42).

James, brother of John, killed by Herod (Acts 12:1-2).

The sons of Zebedee called Boanerges—The sons of thunder (Mark 3:17).

John, writer of John's gospel and Revelation.

Philip of Bethsaida, the city of Andrew and Peter (John 1:44).

Bartholomew (Nathanael), in whom was no guile, found by Philip (John 1:44-51).

Thomas, the doubter (John 20:25).

Matthew, the publican (tax collector) writer of Matthew's gospel (Matt. 9:9; 10:3).

James Thaddaeus, Jesus' brother, writer of James.

LEADER OF THE CHURCH AT JERUSALEM (ACTS 12:17; 15:13)

James and Judas were brothers (Luke 6:16).

James and Judas, the sons of Alphaeus (Acts 1:13), implies that Mary married Alphaeus Thaddaeus, the father of Jesus' brothers James and Judas, who became his disciples (Matt. 10:3; 27:56; Mark 15:40).

Judas Thaddaeus (Lebbaeus Thaddaeus, also Jude), Jesus' brother, writer of Jude.

Simon Zelotes, (Luke 6:15; Acts 1:13); The Canaanite (Matt. 10:4; Mark 3:18).

Judas Iscariot, son of Simon the leper, fell by transgression (Matt. 26:6; John 13; 2; Acts 1:25).

Mathias, chosen by lot by the eleven, replaced Judas Iscariot (Acts 1:1-26).

Behold the Lamb of God, which taketh away the sin of the world (John 1:29).

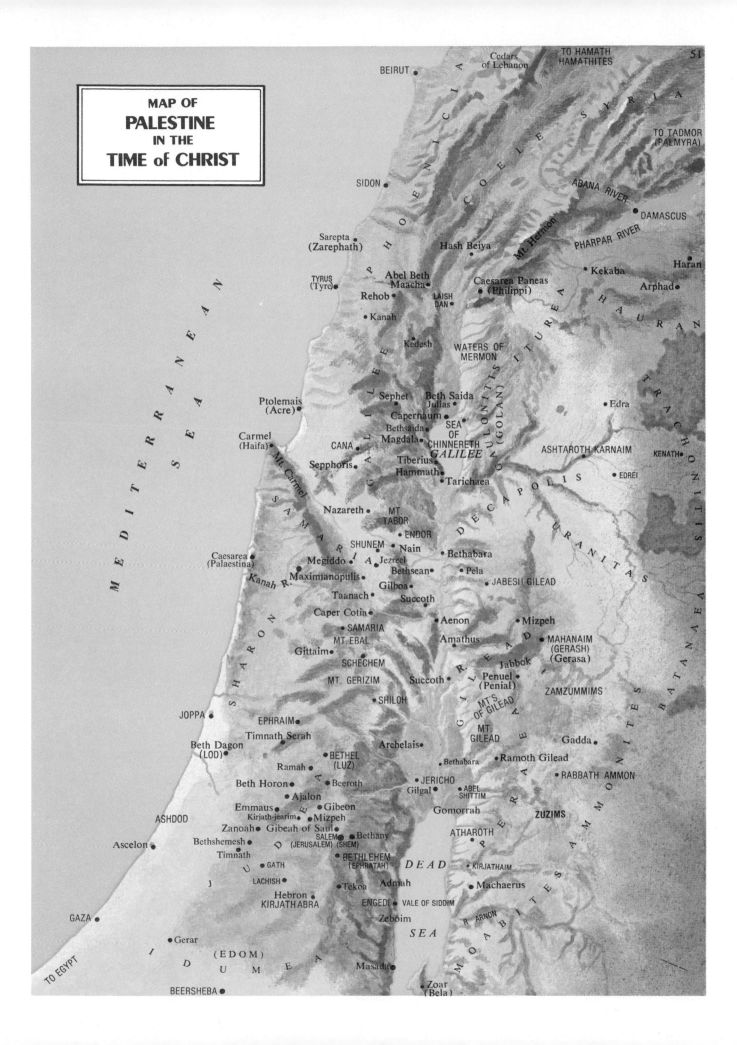

MAP OF
PALESTINE
IN THE
TIME of CHRIST

AD

AM

YOR

TIBERIUS CEASAR

HEROD ANTIPAS

PILATE

LYSANIAS

PHILIP

JULIEN CALENDAR

HEROD'S TEMPLE

Luke (Lucius of Cyrene Acts 13:1; Rom. 16:21; Col. 4:14). The beloved physician was Paul's personal physician from the time they met in Antioch, until Paul's martyrdom. He evangelized the Grecians at Antioch (Acts 11:19-20), and was named among the prophets and teachers (Acts 13:1). He could well have been a descendant of a Levitical family driven to Cyrene in the dispersion of Israel in 721 B.C. (page 41). A Levitical priest was to teach the Word of God (Lev. 10:11; Deut. 24:8,;33:8-10; 2 Chr. 17:9; 30:22; Neh. 8:9; Jer. 18:18; Mal. 2:4-7). Luke was a teacher and physician in Jerusalem before he was driven out because of the persecution that arose about Stephen (Acts 11:19-20). Luke authored his gospel, and The Acts, and helped write 2 Corinthians for Paul.

From the beginning, Luke was an eyewitness and minister of the Word of God, having had perfect understanding of all things from the very first (Luke 1:2-3; Acts 1:1). Luke lists the genealogy of Christ back to Adam, so had to be a learned man, speaking with authority to a man in authority, the most excellent Theophilus (Luke 1:3). It appears that Luke was in Jerusalem during the day of atonement, when the angel of the Lord appeared to Zacharias, since he tells us of the nativity of John the Baptist, and of Jesus (Luke 1, 2; page 48). The "we" in Luke 24:21 tells us Luke, the eyewitness, went to Emmaus with Cleopas (Luke 24:13-35; page 59).

AD

AM

YOR

TIBERIUS CEASAR

HEROD ANTIPAS

PILATE

LYSANIAS

PHILIP

JULIEN CALENDAR

HEROD'S TEMPLE

LUKE'S STORY OF JESUS

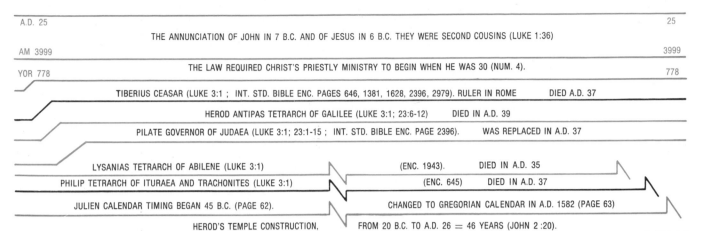

A.D. 25   25

THE ANNUNCIATION OF JOHN IN 7 B.C. AND OF JESUS IN 6 B.C. THEY WERE SECOND COUSINS (LUKE 1:36)

AM 3999   3999

THE LAW REQUIRED CHRIST'S PRIESTLY MINISTRY TO BEGIN WHEN HE WAS 30 (NUM. 4).

YOR 778   778

TIBERIUS CEASAR (LUKE 3:1 ; INT. STD. BIBLE ENC. PAGES 646, 1381, 1628, 2396, 2979). RULER IN ROME   DIED A.D. 37

HEROD ANTIPAS TETRARCH OF GALILEE (LUKE 3:1; 23:6-12)   DIED IN A.D. 39

PILATE GOVERNOR OF JUDAEA (LUKE 3:1; 23:1-15 ; INT. STD. BIBLE ENC. PAGE 2396).   WAS REPLACED IN A.D. 37

LYSANIAS TETRARCH OF ABILENE (LUKE 3:1)   (ENC. 1943).   DIED IN A.D. 35

PHILIP TETRARCH OF ITURAEA AND TRACHONITES (LUKE 3:1)   (ENC. 645)   DIED IN A.D. 37

JULIEN CALENDAR TIMING BEGAN 45 B.C. (PAGE 62).   CHANGED TO GREGORIAN CALENDAR IN A.D. 1582 (PAGE 63)

HEROD'S TEMPLE CONSTRUCTION,   FROM 20 B.C. TO A.D. 26 = 46 YEARS (JOHN 2 :20).

CHRONOLOGICAL HARMONY OF THE GOSPELS

YEARS		EVENTS	PLACE	TIME	MATTHEW	MARK	LUKE	JOHN
JESUS LIFE	JOHN'S LIFE	PRE-EXISTENCE OF CHRIST GENEALOGIES	— —	— —	1:1-17	— —	3:23-28	1:1-18 — —
	7 B.C.	AN ANGEL OF THE LORD APPEARED TO ZACHARIAS	JERUSALEM	OCT. 10, 7th MO. SEE PAGE 48	— —	— —	1:5-25	— —
6 B.C.		THE ANGEL GABRIEL'S ANNUNCIATION TO MARY	NAZARETH	JULY, 4th MO.	— —	— —	1:26-38	— —
		MARY VISITS COUSIN ELIZABETH IN JUDEA	JUDEAN HILLS	JULY—SEPT.	— —	— —	1:39-56	— —
		THE ANGEL, GABRIEL, APPEARED UNTO JOSEPH	NAZARETH	SEPT., 6th MO.	1:18-25	— —	— —	— —
		THE BIRTH OF JOHN TO ZACHARIAS AND ELIZABETH	JUDEAN HILLS	SEPT., 6th MO.	— —	— —	1:57-80	— —
5 B.C.		THE BIRTH OF JESUS. THE SHEPHERDS	BETHLEHEM	APRIL 1, 1st MO.	1:18-25	— —	2:1-20	— —
		CIRCUMCISION OF JESUS	BETHLEHEM	APRIL 8, 1st MO.	— —	— —	2:21	— —
		PURIFICATION LAW (LEV. 12; PAGE 16) RETURN TO NAZARETH	JERUSALEM	MAY 19, 2nd MO.	— —	— —	2:22,39	— —
4 B.C.		WISE MEN FROM THE EAST, OF THE BABYLONIAN CAPTIVITY (2 KI. 25:8-21; LEV. 25), SEEK THEIR MESSIAH	JERUSALEM FROM NAZARETH	UNDER 2 YEARS	2:1-12	— —	2:39	— —
		JOSEPH, MARY, AND JESUS' FLIGHT INTO EGYPT		MAR. MATT. 2:16	2:13-18	— —	2:39	— —
		HEROD THE GREAT DIED ABOUT MARCH 13, 4 B.C.	JERUSALEM	MAR. 12th MO.	2:19-23	— —	— —	— —
3 B.C.		JESUS' CHILDHOOD AND YOUTH	NAZARETH		2:19-23	— —	2:39-40	— —
A.D. 8		JESUS WAS NOW 12 YEARS OF AGE BEFORE THE PASSOVER OF A.D. 8 AM 3982	JERUSALEM	APRIL 1, 1st MO.	— —	— —	2:41-52	— —
A.D. 25	A.D. 25 MINISTRY BEGAN	JOHN WAS SENT FROM GOD WHEN 30 YEARS OLD	JUDAEA	C APRIL	— —	— —	3:1-2	1:6-34
		THE MINISTRY OF JOHN THE BAPTIST BEGAN IN THE WILDERNESS OF JUDAEA	JUDAEA	C SEPT.	3:1-12	1:1-18	3:1-18	— —
		JESUS WAS BAPTIZED BY JOHN	JORDAN	6th MO.	3:13-17	1:9-11	3:21-23	— —
		JOHN'S TESTIMONY OF JESUS	BETHABARA		— —	— —	— —	1:19-34
MINISTRY BEGAN		THE 40-DAY TEMPTATION OF JESUS IN THE WILDERNESS	JUDAEA		4:1-11	1:12-13	4:1-13	— —
		JESUS' FIRST MIRACLE, WATER TO WINE	CANA		— —	— —	— —	2:1-12
		JESUS' RETURN TO THE SEA OF GALILEE	GALILEE		— —	— —	4:14-15	— —
		THIS DAY IS THIS SCRIPTURE FULFILLED IN YOUR EARS. JESUS, A READER IN THE SYNAGOGUE	NAZARETH		— —	— —	4:16-27	— —
		JESUS WAS THRUST OUT FROM NAZARETH	NAZARETH		4:13-17	1:21-28	4:28-37	— —
		SIMON PETER'S MOTHER-IN-LAW WAS HEALED	CAPERNAUM		8:14-17	1:29-34	4:38-41	— —
		JESUS' FIRST DISCIPLES WERE SELECTED	SEA OF GALILEE		4:18-22	1:16-20	5:1-11	1:35-51
		JESUS AND HIS DISCIPLES BEGIN THEIR MINISTRY	GALILEE		4:23-24	1:35-39	4:42-44	— —
		JESUS HEALS THE LEPER	GALILEE		8:2-4	1:40-45	5:12-16	— —
		THE SICK OF THE PALSY WAS LET DOWN THRU THE ROOF	CAPERNAUM		9:2-8	2:1-12	5:17-26	— —
		MATTHEW, CALLED LEVI, BECAME A DISCIPLE	CAPERNAUM		9:9-17	2:13-22	5:27-39	— —
		DISCIPLES PLUCK CORN ON THE SABBATH. JESUS LORD OF SABBATH	CAPERNAUM		12:1-8	2:23-38	6:1-5	— —
		A WITHERED HAND WAS HEALED ON THE SABBATH	CAPERNAUM		12:9-14	3:1-6	6:6-11	— —
		CALLING OF THE TWELVE DISCIPLES (NAMED APOSTLES)	CAPERNAUM NEAR		10:2-4 CH'S.	3:13-19	6:12-19	— —
		SERMON ON THE MOUNT OF BEATITUDES	CAPERNAUM NEAR		5, 6, 7	— —	6:20-49	— —
		I AM COME TO FULFILL ALL THE LAW OF GOD	CAPERNAUM		5:17-18	— —	16:17	— —
		THE CENTURION'S SERVANT WAS HEALED OF PALSY	CAPERNAUM		8:5-13	— —	7:1-10	— —
		THE WIDOW'S SON RAISED FROM THE DEAD	NAIN	12th MO.	— —	— —	7:11-17	— —
		JOHN SENDS HIS DISCIPLES TO JESUS	BETHSAIDA	MARCH	11:2-24	— —	7:18-35	— —

A.D. 26

AM 4000

YOR 779

FROM THE CREATION OF ADAM, WHO WAS CREATED MATURE, TO THE ANOINTING OF THE MATURE MESSIAH WAS 4000 YEARS

A.D. 27

AM 4001

780

TIBERIUS CEASAR RULER IN ROME (LUKE 3:1)DIED MAR.16,A.D.37
(INT. STD. BIBLE ENC. PAGES 646, 1381, 1626, 2396, 2979)

HEROD ANTIPAS TETRARCH OF GALILEE   (LUKE 3:1; 23:6-12)

PILATE GOVERNOR OF JUDAEA (LUKE 3:1; 23:1-15)

(ENC. PAGE 2396).

A.D. 26
AM 4000

Then said the Jews Forty, and six years was this temple in building, and wilt thou rear it up in three days (John 2:20)?

A.D. 26

Jesus, now full 30 years of age, comes to Jerusalem for His first passover when He was of priesthood age. Jesus first priestly service was to cleanse the temple (John 2:13-17). (Compare Num. 4:3, 23, 30, 35, 39, 43;1Chr. 23:3).

CHRONOLOGICAL HARMONY OF THE GOSPELS

YEARS		EVENTS	PLACE	TIME	MATTHEW	MARK	LUKE	JOHN
A.D. 26	JOHN'S MINISTRY	JESUS WAS NOW FULL 30 YEARS OF AGE	JERUSALEM	April 1st, A.D. 26	——	——	——	2:13-25
		JESUS CLEANSES THE TEMPLE (SEE EZEK. 45:18)	JERUSALEM	1st MO.	——	——	——	2:14-17
		HEROD'S TEMPLE WAS 46 YEARS IN BUILDING	JERUSALEM		——	——	——	2:18-25
		NICODEMUS' QUESTION ABOUT THE NEW BIRTH	JERUSALEM		——	——	——	3:1-21
		JOHN CONTINUES BAPTIZING IN JUDAEA	AENON		——	——	——	3:22-27
		JOHN TESTIFIES THAT HE MUST DECREASE	NEAR SALIM		——	——	——	3:26-36
		THE UNPARDONABLE SIN	JERUSALEM		12:31-32	3:22-30	12:10	——
		JESUS LEAVES JERUSALEM FOR GALILEE	THRU SAMARIA		4:12-17	1:14-15	——	4:1-3
		THE WOMAN OF SAMARIA, WHO HAD FIVE HUSBANDS	JACOB'S WELL		——	——	——	4:4-42
		THE NOBELMAN'S SON WAS HEALED	CANA		——	——	——	4:43-54
		THE WARNINGS AGAINST SINFUL CHORAZIN	GALILEE		11:20-30	——	——	——
		WASHING WITH TEARS, ANOINTING WITH OINTMENT, OF JESUS FEET	NAIN		——	——	7:36-50	——
		PARABLE OF THE SOWER	CAPERNAUM		13:1-23	4:1-25	8:1-18	——
		JESUS' MOTHER AND TWO OF HIS BRETHREN WITHOUT ASK FOR HIM		12th MO.	——	(3:16-19	——	——
		JAMES AND JUDAS (APOSTLES) WERE IN THE HOUSE WITH JESUS ..	CAPERNAUM	MARCH	12:46-50	3:31-35)	8:19-21	(P. 50)
A.D. 27		JESUS' SECOND PASSOVER AT JERUSALEM	JERUSALEM	APRIL 14-21	——	——	——	5:1
		JESUS HEALS THE IMPOTENT AT POOL OF BETHESDA	JERUSALEM	1st MO.	——	——	——	5:2-9
		JESUS REVEALS HIMSELF AS THE SON OF GOD	JERUSALEM		——	——	——	5:10-38
		EVEN THE WINDS AND WATER OBEY JESUS	GALILEE		8:18-27	4:35-41	8:22-25	——
		THE DEMONIAC OF GADARA HEALED	GADARA		8:28-34	5:1-21	8:26-39	——
		JAIRUS' DAUGHTER WAS RAISED TO LIFE	CAPERNAUM		9:18-26	5:21-43	8:40-56	——
		TWO BLIND MEN WERE HEALED	CAPERNAUM		9:27-34	——	——	——
		A PROPHET IS NOT WITHOUT HONOR, SAVE IN HIS OWN COUNTRY ..	NAZARETH		13:53-58	6:1-6	——	——
		JESUS SENDS HIS DISCIPLES TO HEAL, AND PREACH SALVATION ...	GALILEE		9:35-11:1	6:6-13	9:1-6	——
		IMPRISONMENT OF JOHN THE BAPTIST	MACHAERUS		14:3-5 14:1-2, 6-12	6:17-20 6:14-16, 21-29	3:19-20	——
		JOHN THE BAPTIST WAS BEHEADED BY HEROD	MACHAERUS				9:7-9	——
		FEEDING OF THE FIVE THOUSAND (5000)	BETHSAIDA	MARCH	14:13-21	6:30-46	9:10-17	6:1-15
		JOHN THE BAPTIST'S MINISTRY ENDS AT AGE 32	MACHAERUS	12th MO.				

JESUS WAS RAISED VERY EARLY THE THIRD DAY. ANY PART OF A DAY IS COUNTED FOR A FULL DAY.

TIBERIUS CAESAR, RULER IN ROME	LUKE 3:1	(ENC. PAGES 646, 1381, 1628, 2396, 2979).		DIED MAR. 16	A.D. 37 AM 4011	
HEROD ANTIPAS	TETRARCH OF GALILEE	LUKE 3:1	LUKE 23:6-12	DIED IN	A.D. 39 AM 4013	
PILATE GOVERNOR OF JUDAEA	LUKE 3:1	LUKE 23:1-15	ENC. 2396	REPLACED IN	A.D. 37 AM 4011	

CHRONOLOGICAL HARMONY OF THE GOSPELS

A.D. 28 EVENTS	PLACE	TIME	MATTHEW	MARK	LUKE	JOHN
Jesus' third passover	Jerusalem	April 14-21	—	—	—	6:4
Jesus walks on the water	Galilee	April	14:22-33	6:47-52	—	6:16-21
As many as touched Jesus' garments were made whole	Gennesaret		14:34-36	6:53-56	—	—
The bread I give is my flesh for the life of the world. From this hard saying, many disciples turn from following Jesus	Capernaum		—	—	—	6:22-71
He that curseth father on mother let him die	Capernaum		15:1-20	7:1-23	—	—
Daughter of the Syrophenician woman healed	Near Sidon		15:21-28	7:24-30	—	—
The deaf and dumb both spoke and heard	Decapolis		15:29-31	7:31-37	—	—
Feeding of the four thousand (4000)	Decapolis		15:32-39	8:1-10	—	—
Beware of the Pharisees and Sadducees who demand signs	Magdala (Dalmanutha)		16:1-12	8:11-21	—	—
Blind man saw men as trees walking	Bethsaida		—	8:22-26	—	—
Peter's confession of faith in Jesus	Caesarea Philippi		16:13-20	8:27-30	9:18-21	—
Jesus foretells how He must suffer of the chief priests, elders, and scribes. Must be killed and be raised the third day	Caesarea Philippi		16:21-28	8:31-9:1	9:22-27	—
Jesus was transfigured before Peter, James, and John	Mt. Tabor		17:1-13	9:2-13	9:28-36	—
The son, demoniac from childhood, was healed	Philippi		17:14-21	9:14-29	9:37-43	—
Jesus, again, foretells of His death and resurrection. They shall kill Him, and the third day He shall be raised	Galilee		17:22-23	9:30-32	9:43-45	—
The fish Peter caught held the tribute money for Jesus and himself	Capernaum		17:24-27	—	—	—
To be great in heaven, become as a child, in faith	Capernaum		18:1-14	9:33-50	9:46-50	—
The feast of Tabernacles	Jerusalem	Oct. 14-22	—	—	—	7:1-10
Shall not Christ come of David, out of Bethlehem, not Galilee?	Jerusalem		—	—	—	7:32-44
A woman taken in adultery. Jesus writes in the sand	Jerusalem		—	—	—	8:3-11
Jesus the light of the world	Jerusalem		—	—	—	8:12-59
Clay and spittle are used to anoint the blind man's eyes	Jerusalem		—	—	—	9:1-39
Jesus, the good Shepherd, laid down His life for His sheep	Jerusalem		—	—	—	10:1-21
Jesus gave His life freely. He had power to lay it down and take it up	Jerusalem		—	—	—	10:17-22
Jesus' warning of the sins of divorce	Judea beyond Jordan		19:1-12	10:2-12	16:18	—
Jesus began preparation for His last trip to Jerusalem	Judea beyond Jordan		—	—	9:51-56	—
Jesus commissioned the seventy disciples for the ministry	Samaria		—	—	10:1-24	—
The first and great Commandment	Near Bethany		—	—	10:25-27	—
The parable of the good Samaritan	Near Bethany		—	—	10:28-37	—
Jesus, a guest of Mary and Martha	Bethany		—	—	10:38-42	—
The Lord's prayer	Mt. of Olives		—	—	11:1-13	—
Beelzebub the prince of devils	Mt. of Olives		12:22-45	—	11:14-23	—
Signs of the times. Yet man can only discern the weather	Mt. of Olives				12:1-59	—
I have a baptism (of death) to be baptized with	Mt. of Olives		20:22	10:38-39	12:49-53	—
Galileans' blood mixed with sacrifices. Parables of fig trees, mustard seed, leaven. Strive to enter the strait gate	Mt. of Olives		—	—	13:1-33	—
Do cures today and tomorrow and the third day be perfected	Mt. of Olives		—	—	13:32	—
Jesus laments over Jerusalem, that killed the prophets	Mt. of Olives		23:37-39	—	13:34-35	—
Feast of dedication or Purim of Esther's decree (page 23)	Jerusalem	Dec. 14-15	—	—	—	10:22-39
Jesus returns to beyond Jordan	Bethabara		—	—	—	10:40-42
Jesus heals a man with dropsy on the Sabbath	Peraea		—	—	14:1-14	—
The great supper, and the many excuses	Peraea		—	—	14:15-25	—
Sacrifices required to be disciples of Jesus	Peraea		—	—	14:25-35	—
Parable of the lost sheep. The lost coin	Peraea		—	—	15:1-10	—
Parable of the prodigal son	Peraea		—	—	15:11-32	—
Parable of the unjust steward	Peraea	February	—	—	16:1-13	—

A.D. 28		A.D. 29
	A.D. 28, THE SABBATICAL YEAR WHICH PRECEDES THE JUBILEE YEAR OF A.D. 29 (LEV. 25; PAGE 28).	
AM 4002		AM 4003
YOR 781		YOR 782

TIBERIUS CAESAR, RULER IN ROME LUKE 3:1 (ENC. PAGES 646, 1381, 1628, 2396, 2979).	DIED MAR. 16	A.D. 37 AM 4011
HEROD ANTIPAS TETRARCH OF GALILEE LUKE 3:1; LUKE 23:6-12	DIED IN	A.D. 39 AM 4013
PILATE GOVERNOR OF JUDAEA LUKE 3:1 LUKE 23:1-15 (ENC. PAGE 2396).	REPLACED IN	A.D. 37 AM 4011

CHRONOLOGICAL HARMONY OF THE GOSPELS

A.D. 28 / EVENTS	PLACE	TIME	MATTHEW	MARK	LUKE	JOHN
The rich man in hell. Lazarus with Abraham	Peraea	February	— —	— —	16:19-31	— —
Forgive until seventy times seven	Peraea	February	18:15-35	11:25-26	17:1-10	— —
Lazarus, brother of Mary and Martha, was raised from dead	Bethany	February	— —	— —	— —	11:1-46
Caiaphas foretold that Jesus should die for that nation	Jerusalem	February	— —	— —	— —	11:47-54
Healing of the ten lepers	Ephraim in	February	— —	— —	17:11-19	— —
Christ's coming. As it was in the days of Noe	Samaria	February	— —	— —	17:20-37	— —
The Pharisee's and publican's different prayers		March	— —	— —	18:1-14	— —
Whosoever must believe as a child to inherit eternal life		March	19:13-15	10:13-16	18:15-17	— —
The rich young ruler lacked the love of God		March	19:16-30	10:17-31	18:18-30	— —
Parable of the laborers, first and last shared equally		March	20:1-16	— —	— —	— —
All things written by the prophets (1 Peter 1:11) concerning **Jesus' sufferings, death, and His resurrection the third day**	Samaria	March	20:17-19	10:32-34	18:31-34	— —
The ambitious requests of James and John	Near Jericho	March	20:20-28	10:35-45	— —	— —
Blind Bartimaeus was healed	Near Jericho	March	20:29-34	10:46-52	18:35-43	— —
Jesus abides at the house of Zacchaeus	Jericho	March	— —	— —	19:1-10	— —
Parable of the profitable and unprofitable servants	Near Jerusalem	March	— —	— —	19:11-28	— —
A.D. 29 The Jews' concern about Jesus' arrival for this passover	Jerusalem	**APRIL 1ST**	— —	— —	— —	11:55-57
Jesus was anointed before His burial, by Mary, six days before the passover	Bethany	Fri. April 8th	— —	— —	— —	12:1-11
The next day, Jesus triumphal entry into Jerusalem	Jerusalem	Sat. April 9th	21:1-11	11:1-11	19:29-44	12:12-19
Jesus cleanses the temple of Sabbath breaking	Jerusalem	Sat. 9th	21:12-17	11:15-19	19:45-48	— —
In the morning, Jesus curses the fig tree	Jerusalem	Sun. 10th	21:18-22	11:12-14, 20-26	— —	— —
The chief priests and elders question Jesus' authority	Temple	Sun. 10th	21:23-27	11:27-33	20:1-8	— —
Publicans and harlots go into God's kingdom before you	Temple	Sun. 10th	21:28-32	— —	— —	— —
Parable of the wicked husbandmen	Temple	Sun. 10th	21:33-46	12:1-12	20:9-19	— —
Parable of the man without a wedding garment	Temple	Sun. 10th	22:1-14	— —	— —	— —
Jesus was questioned about tribute money to Caesar	Temple	Sun. 10th	22:15-22	12:13-17	20:20-26	— —
The Sadducees question about marriage in the resurrection	Temple	Mon. 11th	22:23-33	12:18-27	20:27-40	— —
The great commandment and the second like unto it	Temple	Mon. 11th	22:34-40	12:28-34	— —	— —
What think ye of Christ?	Temple	Mon. 11th	22:41-46	12:35-37	20:41-44	— —
Woes pronounced against the scribes and Pharisees	Temple	Mon. 11th	23:1-36	12:38-40	20:45-47	— —
The widow's mite	Temple	Mon. 11th	— —	12:41-44	21:1-4	— —
Prophecies of the end of the world	Mt. of Olives	Tue. 12th	24:1-51	13:1-37	21:5-36	— —
Parable of the ten virgins	Mt. of Olives	Tue. 12th	25:1-13	— —	— —	— —
Parable of the talents	Mt. of Olives	Tue. 12th	25:14-30	— —	— —	— —
The last judgment foretold	Mt. of Olives	Tue. 12th	25:31-46	— —	— —	— —
The chief priests consult to take Jesus by subtilty	Temple	Tue. 12th	26:3-5	— —	— —	— —
After two days was to be the passover	Temple	Tue. 12th	26:1-2	14:1-2	— —	— —
The chief priests plot with Judas to betray Jesus	Temple	Wed. 13th	26:14-16	14:10-11	22:1-6	— —
The anointing of Jesus at Simon the leper's house. Simon was Judas Iscariot's father (John 12:4)	Bethany	Wed. 13th	26:6-13	14:3-9	— —	— —
The Greeks seek Jesus	Jerusalem	Wed. 13th	— —	— —	— —	12:20-27
For this cause came I unto this hour	Jerusalem	Wed. 13th	— —	— —	— —	12:27
God spoke to Jesus for all the people to hear, **promising to glorify Him again**	Jerusalem	Wed. 13th	— —	— —	— —	12:28-30
Jesus foretells the prince of this world to be cast out. That great dragon was cast out (Rev. 12:7-12)	Jerusalem	Wed. 13th	— —	— —	10:18	12:30-31
Jesus signifies by what death He should die. **He must be lifted up (on the cross)**	Jerusalem	Wed. 13th	— —	— —	— —	12:32-50

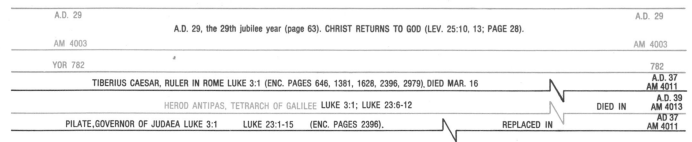

A.D. 29		A.D. 29
	A.D. 29, the 29th jubilee year (page 63). CHRIST RETURNS TO GOD (LEV. 25:10, 13; PAGE 28).	
AM 4003		AM 4003
YOR 782		782

TIBERIUS CAESAR, RULER IN ROME LUKE 3:1 (ENC. PAGES 646, 1381, 1628, 2396, 2979). DIED MAR. 16 — A.D. 37 AM 4011

HEROD ANTIPAS, TETRARCH OF GALILEE LUKE 3:1; LUKE 23:6-12 — DIED IN — A.D. 39 AM 4013

PILATE, GOVERNOR OF JUDAEA LUKE 3:1   LUKE 23:1-15   (ENC. PAGES 2396). — REPLACED IN — AD 37 AM 4011

CHRONOLOGICAL HARMONY OF THE GOSPELS

A.D. 29	EVENTS	PLACE	TIME	MATTHEW	MARK	LUKE	JOHN
	Preparation for the passover. The 1st day of unleavened bread	Jerusalem	Thur. April 14th	26:17-19	14:12-16	22:7-13	— —
	Arrival at the upper room	Jerusalem	Thur. 14th	26:20	14:17	22:14	— —
	The last supper. "With desire I have desired to eat it."	Upper Room	Thur. 14th	26:26-29	14:22-25	22:15-20	1 Cor. 11:23-26

THE LAST SUPPER   JESUS WASHING THE DISCIPLES FEET   PETER IN CAIAPHAS' PALACE

EVENTS	PLACE	TIME	MATTHEW	MARK	LUKE	JOHN
Jesus washes the disciples' feet	Upper Room	Thur. April 14th	— —	— —	— —	13:1-20
Judas Iscariot, identified as Jesus' betrayer	Upper Room	Thur. 14th	26:21-25	14:18-21	22:21-23	13:21-35
That thou (Judas) doest, do quickly	Upper Room	Thur. 14th	— —	— —	— —	13:26-27
Strife for precedence among the disciples	Upper Room	Thur. 14th	— —	— —	22:24-30	— —
Before the cock crow, Peter would deny Jesus thrice	Upper Room	Thur. 14th	— —	— —	22:31-38	13:36-38
The lamb slain from the foundation of the world (Rev. 13:8)	Upper Room	Thur. 14th	— —	— —	22:37	1:29, 36
Farewell of Jesus to His disciples	Upper Room	Thur. 14th	— —	— —	— —	Ch's. 14-18
Ye shall be scattered, yet I am not alone	Upper Room	Thur. 14th	26:31	14:27	— —	16:32-33
Jesus prays for His disciples	Upper Room	Thur. 14th	— —	— —	— —	Chap. 17
Jesus and His disciples cross Cidron to Gethsemane	Gethsemane	Thur. 14th	26:30-32	14:26-28	22:39	18:1-2
Peter vows not to be offended because of Jesus	Gethsemane	Thur. 14th	26:33-35	14:29-31	— —	— —
Sufferings of Jesus in Gethsemane. "Let this cup pass from me" ...	Gethsemane	Thur. 14th	26:36-46	14:32-42	22:40-46	18:1-2
"My soul is exceeding sorrowful even unto death" Jesus sweat as it were great drops of blood (see Isa. 52:14)	Gethsemane	Thur. 14th	26:38	14:34	22:44	(Heb. 9:22)
Thursday night was the beginning of Jesus' passion	Gethsemane	Thur. 14th	12:40	[Jonah's sufferings page 59,62]		
An angel strengthens Jesus ". . . The hour is at hand"	Gethsemane	Thur. 14th	26:45-46	14:35	22:43	16:32
"I have finished the work thou gavest one to do"	Gethsemane	Thur. 14th	— —	— —	— —	17:1, 4, 13
Judas' betrayal of Jesus in Gethsemane	Gethsemane	Thur. 14th	26:47-50	14:43-45	22:47-48	18:3-9
Peter smote off the ear of Malchus, servant of the high priest	Gethsemane	Thur. 14th	26:51-52	14:46-48	22:49-51	18:10-11
Jesus could have had twelve legions of Angels	Gethsemane	Thur. 14th	26:53	— —	— —	— —
I sat daily with you in the temple	Gethsemane	Thur. 14th	26:55	— —	21:37	— —
The arrest of Jesus	Gethsemane	Late evening	26:50-56	14:46-52	22:49-54	18:10-12
Jesus before Annas, the father of Caiaphas	Jerusalem	Midnight	— —	— —	— —	18:13-15
Preparation day, Friday, the day before the Sabbath	Jerusalem	Fri. April 15th	27:62	15:42	— —	19:14, 31, 42
Jesus before Caiaphas, and the scribes and elders	Caiaphas Palace	Fri. 15th	26:57-66	14:53-64	22:54	
Jesus visage was marred more than any man (Isa. 52:14). Jesus was spit upon, and buffeted. He was wounded for our transgressions (Isa. 53:5)	Caiaphas Palace	Before Daylight	26:67-68	14:65	22:63-71	18:19-24
Peter's denials. Peter a witness to Christ's sufferings (1 Peter 5:1)..	Caiaphas Palace	Before Daylight	26:69-75	14:66-72	22:55-62	18:15-18, 25-27

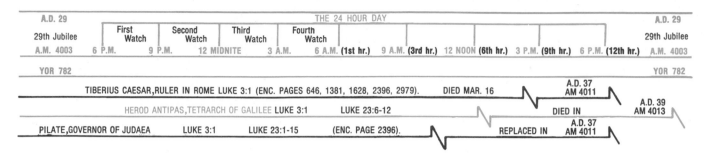

A.D. 29				THE 24 HOUR DAY								A.D. 29
29th Jubilee	First Watch	Second Watch	Third Watch	Fourth Watch								29th Jubilee
A.M. 4003	6 P.M.	9 P.M.	12 MIDNITE	3 A.M.	6 A.M. (1st hr.)	9 A.M. (3rd hr.)	12 NOON (6th hr.)	3 P.M. (9th hr.)	6 P.M. (12th hr.)			A.M. 4003
YOR 782												YOR 782

TIBERIUS CAESAR, RULER IN ROME LUKE 3:1 (ENC. PAGES 646, 1381, 1628, 2396, 2979). DIED MAR. 16 A.D. 37 AM 4011

HEROD ANTIPAS, TETRARCH OF GALILEE LUKE 3:1 LUKE 23:6-12 DIED IN A.D. 39 AM 4013

PILATE, GOVERNOR OF JUDAEA LUKE 3:1 LUKE 23:1-15 (ENC. PAGE 2396). REPLACED IN A.D. 37 AM 4011

CHRONOLOGICAL HARMONY OF THE GOSPELS

A.D. 29	EVENTS	PLACE	TIME			MATTHEW	MARK	LUKE	JOHN
	As soon as it was day, Jesus was delivered to Pilate	Judgment Hall in Jerusalem	Fri.	April	15th	27:1-2	15:1	22:66-23.1	——
	Judas returns the 30 pieces of silver and hangs himself (Acts 1:18-19)	Jerusalem	Fri.		15th	27:3-10	——	——	——
	Very early, Caiaphas delivered Jesus to Pilate's Judgment hall. The chief priest s, vehemently, accuse Jesus before Herod and Pilate, though enemies, are now made friends	Jerusalem	Fri.	6 A.M.	15th	27:11-14	15:2-5	23:2-12	18:28-38
	Being a jubilee year, a prisoner must be set free. Pilate pleads for the release of Jesus on this high day (John 19:31). Jesus returned to his father after His resurrection, fulfilling the law (Lev. 25:13; Jer. 34:9, 15-17)	Judgment Hall	Fri.		15th	27:15-23	15:6-14	23:13-17	18:38-40
	Pilate, therefore, scourged Jesus finding no fault in Him. Pilate's soldiers put on Jesus, the crown of thorns, and purple robe	Praetorium	Fri.		15th	27:27-31	15:16-20	23:20-22	19:1-3
	Pilate washes his hands saying, "I am innocent of the blood of this just person." The Jews reply, "His blood be on us and our children"	Judgment Hall	Fri.	To	15th	27:24-30	——	——	——
	Pilate releases Barabbas	Judgment Hall	Fri.		15th	——	15:15	23:25	——
	The Jews demanded Jesus' life, because He claimed to be the Son of God	Judgment Hall	Fri.		15th	——	——	——	19:4-9
	Pilate had no power to release Jesus. He that delivered Jesus to Pilate had the greater sin	Judgment Hall	Fri.		15th	——	——	——	19:10-13
	Jesus was led away to be crucified. "Behold your King." "We have no king but Caesar" (Preparation day)	Jerusalem	Fri.		15th	27:31	15:20	23:25	19:14-15
	Simon of Cyrene helps Jesus bear the cross	to Golgotha	Fri.	9 A.M.	15th	27:32	15:21	23:26	19:16

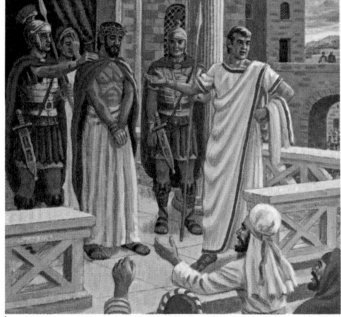

JESUS BEFORE PILATE		THE CRUCIFIXION							
The crucifixion of Jesus was the third hour	Golgotha	Fri.	9 A.M.	15th		15:22-25	[see page 62]		
"Father, forgive them; they know not what they do" The superscription in Greek, Latin, and Hebrew: This is The King of the Jews	Golgotha	Fri.		15th	——	——	23:34	——	
	Golgotha	Fri.		15th	27:37	15:26	23:35-38	19:19-22	
The soldiers cast lots for Jesus' seamless coat (vesture)	Golgotha	Fri.		15th	27:35-36	15:24	23:34	19:23-24	
The priests and Jews mock Jesus, "If thou be the Christ come down from the cross and we will believe"	Golgotha	Fri.		15th	27:39-44	15:29-32	23:35	——	
To the thief, "Today shalt thou be with me in Paradise"	Golgotha	Fri.		15th	27:38	15:27-28	23:39-43	——	
"Mary behold thy son." "John behold thy mother"	Golgotha	Fri. C 11:45 A.M.		15th	——	——	——	19:25-27	

PENTECOST ALWAYS FALLS ON A SUNDAY. THE FIFTIETH DAY AFTER THE SABBATH OF THE PASSOVER WEEK (LEV. 23:10-16; ACTS 2:1; PAGE 23)

59

A.D. 29		A.D. 70
29th Jubilee	The high sabbath was celebrated only during a jubilee year passover (Lev. 25:13; John 19:31).	
AM 4003		AM 4054
YOR 782		YOR 823

HE IS NOT HERE HE IS RISEN

For as Jonas (Jonah) was three days and three nights in the whale's belly; so shall the Son of man be three days and three nights in the heart of the earth (Matt. 12:40; 16:4). Jonah's great sufferings pre-pictured Jesus' sufferings and death. "In the heart of the earth" is symbolic language meaning "suffering and death." Jonah did not go to hell, or die in the belly of the whale, yet he expresses his agonies by saying that he cried out of the belly of hell (Jonah 2:2). The "lower parts of the earth in Eph. 4:9" means "death." Who shall descend into the deep? (That is, to bring up Christ again from the dead) (Rom. 10:7). Jesus and the forgiven thief both went to paradise when they died (Luke 23:43) Friday, April 15, A.D. 29. (see pages 40, 57, 62).

The third temple at Jerusalem was destroyed by Titus in A.D. 70.

CHRONOLOGICAL HARMONY OF THE GOSPELS

A.D. 29	EVENTS	PLACE	TIME			MATTHEW	MARK	LUKE	JOHN
	Darkness over all the land, from the 6th hour (12 Noon)—9th hour (3 P.M.)	all the land	Fri.	12-3 P.M.	15th	27:45	15:33	23:44-45	[Page 58]
	At the ninth hour, Jesus cried, "Eli, Eli, lama sabachthani"	Golgotha	Fri.	3 P.M.	15th	27:46-47	15:34-35	— —	— —
	Jesus cried with a loud voice and gave up the ghost	Golgotha	Fri.	3 P.M.	15th	27:48-49	15:36	23:46	19:28-30
	The veil of the temple, rent top to bottom, typifies Jesus' flesh (Heb. 10:20). The Centurion said "Truly this was the son of God"	Golgotha	Fri.	3 P.M.	15th	27:50-55	15:37-39	23:45-49	— —
	Jesus died on preparation day (Friday) the day before the high sabbath (Saturday). Side pierced, no bone broken	Golgotha	Fri.	3 P.M.	15th	— —	— —	— —	19:31-37
	Pilate marvelled that Jesus was so soon dead. Joseph of Arimathaea buried Jesus, at even, in his own tomb (see Deut. 21:22-23)	Garden	Preparation day			27:57-61	15:42-47	23:50-54	19:38-42
	The sabbath (Saturday) after preparation day, the chief priests and Pharisees asked Pilate to make the sepulchre sure until the 3rd day, lest Jesus' disciples steal Him away; because He had said, "After three days I will rise again"	Garden	Sat.	Sabbath	16th	27:62-64	— —	— —	— —
	Resurrection day, very early upon the first day of the week, Jesus arose as He said on the third day (page 55)	Garden	Sun.	April	17th	28:1-6	16:1-6	24:1-7	20:1
	Mary Magdalene runs to tell Peter and John that Jesus was gone	Garden	Sun.	April	17th				20:1-2
	Ye seek Jesus: He is not here; He is risen	Garden	Sun.		17th	28:5-8	16:5-8	24:3-8	— —
	Peter and John ran to the sepulchre and saw only empty linen	Garden	Sun.		17th	— —	— —	24:12	20:3-10
	Jesus appears to Mary Magdalene before He ascended to His Father	Garden	Sun.		17th	— —	16:9-11	— —	20:11-18
	Pilate's guards are promised security by the chief priests	Jerusalem	Sun.		17th	28:11-15	— —	— —	— —
	Luke and Cleopas converse with Jesus. Luke an eyewitness (Luke 1:2)	Road to Emmaus	Sun.		17th	— —	16:12-13	24:13-25	[Page 52]
	The same day, Jesus appeared to His apostles in the upper room	Jerusalem	Sun.		17th	28:9-10	16:14-18	24:26-53	20:19-25
	After 8 days, Jesus appears to all His apostles, including Thomas	Jerusalem	Sun.	April	24th	— —			20:26-31
	The third time after Jesus' resurrection. He appears to His disciples at Sea of Galilee, where they went fishing	Sea of Galilee		April		28:16-20	— —		21:1-14
	Simon lovest thou me more than these (disciples)?	Sea of Galilee		April		— —	— —	— —	21:15-17
	Jesus foretells the manner of Peter's martyrdom	Sea of Galilee		April		— —	— —	— —	21:18-25
	The Great Commission: "Go ye . . ."	Galilee		April		28:19	16:15	— —	15:16
	The Ascension, after being seen of them 40 days (April 17-May 26)	Mt. of Olives	Friday	May	26	— —	16:19-20	24:49-53	(Acts 1:3, 9-12)
	Pentecost Sunday came 50 days after the passover sabbath	Jerusalem	Sun. June 5 A.D. 29			[Lev. 23:11, 15-16; Deut. 16:9, Pages 23, 60, 62]			
	Jesus appeared to Paul near Damascus	Damascus	C-A.D. 35			— —	— —	Acts 22:6-16	
	Jesus reveals the Revelation to John on the Isle of Patmos	Patmos	C-A.D. 68			— —	— —	— —	Rev. 1:9-20
	Jesus, our High Priest, in Heaven (Heb. 6:20; 9:11-28)	with His Father	Sun. April 17, A.D. 29			— —	— —	— —	
	The new heaven and the new earth	new earth	Future			— —	— —	— —	Rev. 21:1-21

TONGUES OF FIRE FILLED ALL THE HOUSE

JAMES THE LEADER OF THE CHURCH AT JERUSALEM

PENTECOST

But ye shall receive power, after that the Holy Ghost is come upon you: and ye shall be witnesses unto me both in Jerusalem, and in all Judea, and in Samaria, and unto the uttermost part of the earth (Acts 1:8).

JAMES, THE BROTHER OF JESUS

James, the brother of Jesus, the leader of the church at Jerusalem (Acts 12:17; 15:13, 19). Read Acts 21:1-18; 15:6-35 .

ASCENSION

JESUS GOING TO THE HEAVENLY HOME

. . . this same Jesus which is taken up from you into heaven shall so come in like manner as ye have seen him go into heaven (Acts 1:11 . ; read Matt. 24; Mark 13; Luke 17:26-37; 2 Thess. 2).

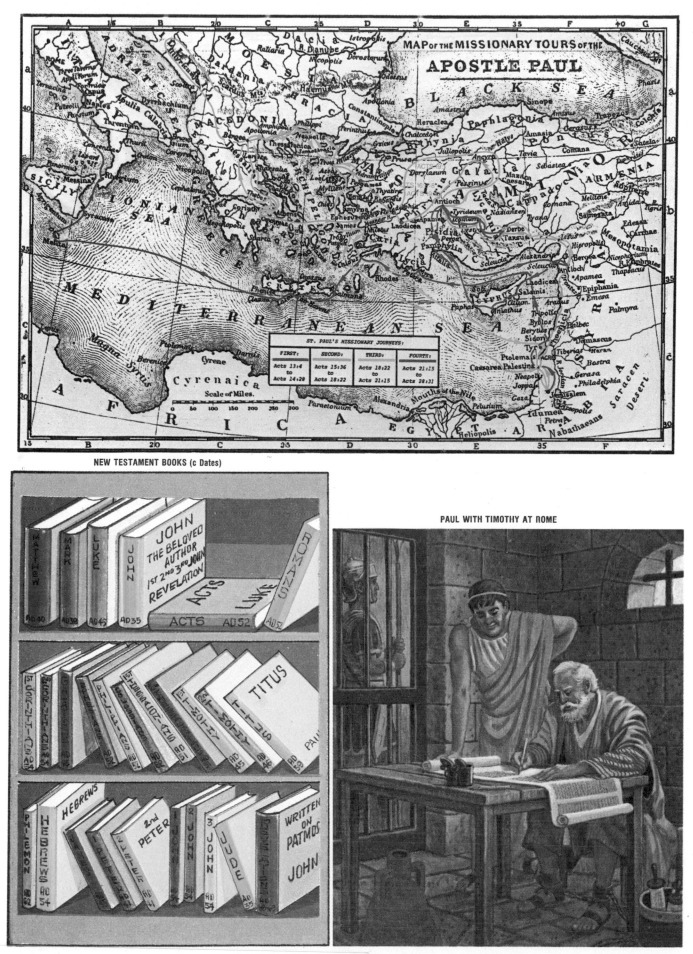

MAP of the MISSIONARY TOURS of the

APOSTLE PAUL

ST. PAUL'S MISSIONARY JOURNEYS:			
FIRST:	SECOND:	THIRD:	FOURTH:
Acts 13:4 to Acts 14:28	Acts 15:36 to Acts 18:22	Acts 18:22 to Acts 21:15	Acts 21:15 to Acts 28:31

NEW TESTAMENT BOOKS (c Dates)

PAUL WITH TIMOTHY AT ROME

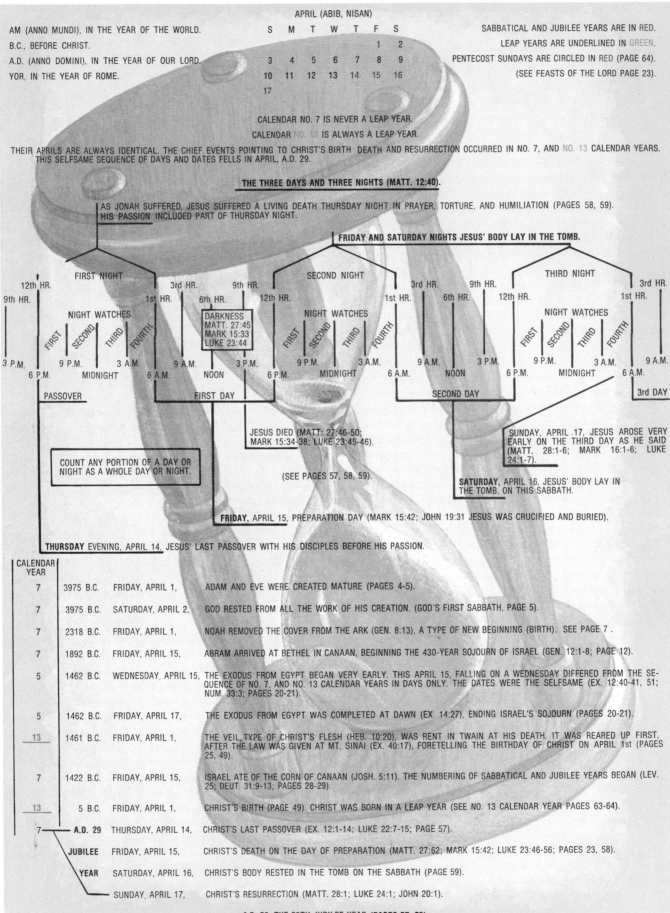

AM (ANNO MUNDI), IN THE YEAR OF THE WORLD.
B.C., BEFORE CHRIST.
A.D. (ANNO DOMINI), IN THE YEAR OF OUR LORD.
YOR, IN THE YEAR OF ROME.

APRIL (ABIB, NISAN)

S	M	T	W	T	F	S
					1	2
3	4	5	6	7	8	9
10	11	12	13	14	15	16
17						

SABBATICAL AND JUBILEE YEARS ARE IN RED.
LEAP YEARS ARE UNDERLINED IN GREEN.
PENTECOST SUNDAYS ARE CIRCLED IN RED (PAGE 64).
(SEE FEASTS OF THE LORD PAGE 23).

CALENDAR NO. 7 IS NEVER A LEAP YEAR.

CALENDAR NO. 13 IS ALWAYS A LEAP YEAR.

THEIR APRILS ARE ALWAYS IDENTICAL. THE CHIEF EVENTS POINTING TO CHRIST'S BIRTH DEATH AND RESURRECTION OCCURRED IN NO. 7, AND NO. 13 CALENDAR YEARS. THIS SELFSAME SEQUENCE OF DAYS AND DATES FELLS IN APRIL, A.D. 29.

THE THREE DAYS AND THREE NIGHTS (MATT. 12:40).

AS JONAH SUFFERED, JESUS SUFFERED A LIVING DEATH THURSDAY NIGHT IN PRAYER, TORTURE, AND HUMILIATION (PAGES 58, 59). HIS PASSION INCLUDED PART OF THURSDAY NIGHT.

FRIDAY AND SATURDAY NIGHTS JESUS' BODY LAY IN THE TOMB.

DARKNESS
MATT. 27:45
MARK 15:33
LUKE 23:44

COUNT ANY PORTION OF A DAY OR NIGHT AS A WHOLE DAY OR NIGHT.

JESUS DIED (MATT. 27:46-50; MARK 15:34-38; LUKE 23:45-46).

(SEE PAGES 57, 58, 59).

SUNDAY, APRIL .17, JESUS AROSE VERY EARLY ON THE THIRD DAY AS HE SAID (MATT. 28:1-6; MARK 16:1-6; LUKE 24:1-7).

SATURDAY, APRIL 16, JESUS' BODY LAY IN THE TOMB, ON THIS SABBATH.

FRIDAY, APRIL 15, PREPARATION DAY (MARK 15:42; JOHN 19:31 JESUS WAS CRUCIFIED AND BURIED).

THURSDAY EVENING, APRIL 14. JESUS' LAST PASSOVER WITH HIS DISCIPLES BEFORE HIS PASSION.

CALENDAR YEAR			
7	3975 B.C.	FRIDAY, APRIL 1,	ADAM AND EVE WERE CREATED MATURE (PAGES 4-5).
7	3975 B.C.	SATURDAY, APRIL 2,	GOD RESTED FROM ALL THE WORK OF HIS CREATION. (GOD'S FIRST SABBATH, PAGE 5).
7	2318 B.C.	FRIDAY, APRIL 1,	NOAH REMOVED THE COVER FROM THE ARK (GEN. 8:13), A TYPE OF NEW BEGINNING (BIRTH). SEE PAGE 7 .
7	1892 B.C.	FRIDAY, APRIL 15,	ABRAM ARRIVED AT BETHEL IN CANAAN, BEGINNING THE 430-YEAR SOJOURN OF ISRAEL (GEN. 12:1-8; PAGE 12).
5	1462 B.C.	WEDNESDAY, APRIL 15,	THE EXODUS FROM EGYPT BEGAN VERY EARLY. THIS APRIL 15, FALLING ON A WEDNESDAY DIFFERED FROM THE SEQUENCE OF NO. 7, AND NO. 13 CALENDAR YEARS IN DAYS ONLY. THE DATES WERE THE SELFSAME (EX. 12:40-41, 51; NUM. 33:3; PAGES 20-21).
5	1462 B.C.	FRIDAY, APRIL 17,	THE EXODUS FROM EGYPT WAS COMPLETED AT DAWN (EX. 14:27), ENDING ISRAEL'S SOJOURN (PAGES 20-21).
13	1461 B.C.	FRIDAY, APRIL 1,	THE VEIL, TYPE OF CHRIST'S FLESH (HEB. 10:20), WAS RENT IN TWAIN AT HIS DEATH. IT WAS REARED UP FIRST, AFTER THE LAW WAS GIVEN AT MT. SINAI (EX. 40:17), FORETELLING THE BIRTHDAY OF CHRIST ON APRIL 1st (PAGES 25, 49).
7	1422 B.C.	FRIDAY, APRIL 15,	ISRAEL ATE OF THE CORN OF CANAAN (JOSH. 5:11). THE NUMBERING OF SABBATICAL AND JUBILEE YEARS BEGAN (LEV. 25; DEUT. 31:9-13; PAGES 28-29).
13	5 B.C.	FRIDAY, APRIL 1,	CHRIST'S BIRTH (PAGE 49). CHRIST WAS BORN IN A LEAP YEAR (SEE NO. 13 CALENDAR YEAR PAGES 63-64).
7	A.D. 29	THURSDAY, APRIL 14,	CHRIST'S LAST PASSOVER (EX. 12:1-14; LUKE 22:7-15; PAGE 57).
	JUBILEE	FRIDAY, APRIL 15,	CHRIST'S DEATH ON THE DAY OF PREPARATION (MATT. 27:62; MARK 15:42; LUKE 23:46-56; PAGES 23, 58).
	YEAR	SATURDAY, APRIL 16,	CHRIST'S BODY RESTED IN THE TOMB ON THE SABBATH (PAGE 59).
		SUNDAY, APRIL 17,	CHRIST'S RESURRECTION (MATT. 28:1; LUKE 24:1; JOHN 20:1).

A.D. 29, THE 29TH JUBILEE YEAR (PAGES 57, 63).

A.D. LEAP YEARS ARE THE YEARS DIVISIBLE BY FOUR, EXCEPTING FOR CENTENNIAL YEARS WHICH MUST BE DIVISIBLE BY FOUR HUNDRED (SEE PAGE 63).

THE ACCURACY OF THE GREGORIAN CALENDAR BRINGS THE BIBLE DATES THROUGH PERFECTLY FROM ADAM

THE CALENDAR DEVELOPED BY THOTH, AN EGYPTIAN, WHO ENLISTED THE HELP OF SOSIGENES, AN EMINENT EGYPTIAN ASTRONOMER, WAS ADOPTED BY JULIUS CAESAR IN 46 B.C., THE YEAR OF ROME 708. IT BECAME KNOWN AS THE JULIEN CALENDAR TO BE USED FOR THE GENERAL BASIS OF RECKONING (THE BOOKS OF KNOWLEDGE). SEE PAGE 47 .

YEAR OF ROME	B.C.	CAL. NO.	AM
709	45	12	3930
710	44	7	3931
711	43	1	3932
712	42	2	3933
713	41	10	3934
714	40	5	3935
715	39	6	3936
716	38	7	3937
717	37	8	3938
718	36	3	3939
719	35	4	3940
720	34	5	3941
721	33	13	3942
722	32	1	3943
723	31	2	3944
724	30	3	3945
725	29	11	3946
726	28	6	3947
727	27	7	3948
728	26	1	3949
729	25	9	3950
730	24	4	3951
731	23	5	3952
28th JUBILEE YEAR			
732	22	6	3953
733	21	14	3954
734	20	2	3955
735	19	3	3956
736	18	4	3957
737	17	12	3958
738	16	7	3959
739	15	1	3960
740	14	2	3961
741	13	10	3962
742	12	5	3963
743	11	6	3064
744	10	7	3965
745	09	8	3966
746	08	3	3967
747	07	4	3968
748	06	5	3969
749	05	13	3970
JESUS WAS BORN APRIL 1st,5 B.C. THE FIRST MONTH OF THE YEAR, APPROX. 23½ MONTHS BEFORE HEROD THE GREAT DIED. (COMPARE MATT. 2:16).			
750	04	1	3971
HEROD DIED THE 12th MONTH (MARCH) IN THE YOR 750 (PAGE 49).			
751	03	2	3972
752	02	3	3973
BEFORE CHRIST, B.C.			
753	01	12	3974
A 12-MONTH PERIOD			
ANNO	DOMINI		AM
754	01	7	3975
755	02	1	3976
756	03	2	3977
757	04	10	3978
758	05	5	3979
759	06	6	3980
760	07	7	3981
761	08	8	3982
762	09	3	3983
763	10	4	3984
TIBERIUS CAESAR BEGAN HIS REIGN IN ROME LUKE 3:1			
764	11	5	3985
765	12	13	3986
766	13	1	3987
767	14	2	3988
768	15	3	3989
769	16	11	3990
770	17	6	3991
771	18	7	3992
772	19	1	3993
773	20	9	3994
774	21	4	3995
775	22	5	3996

YEAR OF ROME	A.D.	CAL. NO.	AM
776	23	6	3997
777	24	14	3998
778	25	2	3999
69 WEEKS OF YEARS TO THE ANOINTING OF THE MOST HOLY, FULFILLED IN A.D. 25, AT THE BAPTISM OF JESUS BY JOHN (DAN. 9:25) (PAGE 54). JESUS' AGE APPROX. 30 (LUKE 3:23)			
779	26	3	4000
JESUS WAS NOW FULL 30 YEARS OF AGE, PREPARED FOR HIS MINISTRY (COMPARE NUM. 4). FROM ADAM A MATURE MAN, TO CHRIST A MATURE MAN IS 4000 YEARS.			
780	27	4	4001
781	28	12	4002
782	29	7	4003
THE 29th JUBILEE YEAR CRUCIFIXION AND RESURRECTION OF JESUS SEE THE LAW OF JUBILEE (LEV. 25)			
783	30	1	4004
784	31	2	4005
785	32	10	4006
786	33	5	4007
787	34	6	4008
788	35	7	4009
789	36	8	4010
790	37	3	4011
803	50	5	4024
823	70	2	4044
DESTRUCTION OF HEROD'S TEMPLE			
831	78	5	4052
JUBILEE YEAR			
832	79	6	4053
853	100	4	4074
881	128	10	4102
JUBILEE YEAR			
882	129	5	4103
903	150	3	4124
931	178	3	4152
JUBILEE YEAR			
932	179	4	4153
952	200	2	4174
981	228	8	4202
JUBILEE YEAR			
982	229	3	4203
1003	250	1	4224
1031	278	1	4252
JUBILEE YEAR			
1032	279	2	4253
1053	300	7	4274
1081	328	13	4302
JUBILEE YEAR			
1082	329	1	4303
1103	350	6	4324
1131	378	6	4352
JUBILEE YEAR			
1132	379	7	4353
1153	400	12	4374

A.D.	CAL. NO.	AM
428	12	4402
JUBILEE YEAR		
429	7	4403
450	5	4424
478	5	4452
JUBILEE YEAR		
479	6	4453
500	4	4474
528	10	4502
JUBILEE YEAR		
529	5	4503
550	3	4524
578	3	4552
JUBILEE YEAR		
579	4	4553
600	2	4574
628	8	4602
JUBILEE YEAR		
629	3	4603
650	1	4624
678	1	4652
JUBILEE YEAR		
679	2	4653
700	7	4674
728	13	4702
JUBILEE YEAR		
729	1	4703
750	6	4724
778	6	4752
JUBILEE YEAR		
779	7	4753
800	12	4774
828	12	4802
JUBILEE YEAR		
829	7	4803
850	5	4824
878	5	4852
JUBILEE YEAR		
879	6	4853
900	4	4874
928	10	4902
JUBILEE YEAR		
929	5	4903

A.D.	CAL. NO.	AM
950	3	4924
978	3	4952
JUBILEE YEAR		
979	4	4953
1000	2	4974
1028	8	5002
JUBILEE YEAR		
1029	3	5003
1050	1	5024
1078	1	5052
JUBILEE YEAR		
1079	2	5053
1100	7	5074
1128	13	5102
JUBILEE YEAR		
1129	1	5103
1150	6	5124
1178	6	5152
JUBILEE YEAR		
1179	7	5153
1200	12	5174
1228	12	5202
JUBILEE YEAR		
1229	7	5203
1250	5	5224
1278	5	5252
JUBILEE YEAR		
1279	6	5253
1300	4	5274
1328	10	5302
JUBILEE YEAR		
1329	5	5303
1350	3	5324
1378	3	5352
JUBILEE YEAR		
1379	4	5353
1400	2	5374
1428	8	5402
JUBILEE YEAR		
1429	3	5403
1450	1	5424
1478	1	5452

A.D.	CAL. NO.	AM
JUBILEE YEAR		
1479	2	5453
1500	7	5474
1528	13	5502
JUBILEE YEAR		
1529	1	5503
1550	6	5524
1578	6	5552
JUBILEE YEAR		
1579	7	5553
1580	8	5554
1581	3	5555
1582	4	5556
	10th MO.	1st
		2nd
11 DAY PICK-UP →		3rd
		15th
		16th
THE BEGINNING OF THE GREGORIAN CALENDAR BY DECREE OF POPE GREGORY XIII		17th
		18th
		19th
		20th
		21st
		22nd
		23rd
		24th
		25th
		26th
NEXT PICK-UP OF ONE DAY IN A.D. 1905		27th
		28th
		29th
		30th
		31st
1583	7	5557
1584	8	5558
1600	14	5574
1628	14	5602
JUBILEE YEAR		
1629	2	5603
1650	7	5624
1678	7	5652
JUBILEE YEAR		
1679	1	5653
1700	6	5674
1728	12	5702
JUBILEE YEAR		
1729	7	5703
1750	5	5724
1778	5	5752
JUBILEE YEAR		
1779	6	5753
1800	4	5774
1828	10	5792
1850	3	5824

A.D.	CAL. NO.	AM
1870	7	5844
1871	1	5845
1872	9	5846
1873	4	5847
1874	5	5848
1875	6	5849
1876	14	5850
1877	2	5851
1878	3	5852
JUBILEE YEAR		
1879	4	5853
1880	12	5854
1881	7	5855
1882	1	5856
1883	2	5857
1884	10	5858
1885	5	5859
1886	6	5860
1887	7	5861
1888	8	5862
1889	3	5863
1890	4	5864
1891	5	5865
1892	13	5866
1893	1	5867
1894	2	5868
1895	3	5869
1896	11	5870
1897	6	5871
1898	7	5872
1899	1	5873
1900	2	5874
1901	3	5875
1902	4	5876
1903	5	5877
1904	13	5878
1905	1	5879
1006	2	5880
1907	3	5881
1908	11	5882
1909	6	5883
1910	7	5884
1911	1	5885
1912	9	5886
1913	4	5887
1914	5	5888
1915	6	5889
1916	14	5890
1917	2	5891
1918	3	5892
1919	4	5893
1920	12	5894
1921	7	5895
1922	1	5896
1923	2	5897
1924	10	5898
1925	5	5899
1926	6	5900
1927	7	5901
1928	8	5902
JUBILEE YEAR		
1929	3	5903
1930	4	5904
1931	5	5905
1932	13	5906
1933	1	5907
1934	2	5908
1935	3	5909
1936	11	5910
1937	6	5911
1938	7	5912
1939	1	5913
1940	9	5914
1941	4	5915
1942	5	5916
1943	6	5917
1944	14	5918
1945	2	5919
1946	3	5920
1947	4	5921
1948	12	5922
1949	7	5923.
1950	1	5924
1951	2	5925

A.D.	CAL. NO.	AM
1952	10	5926
1953	5	5927
1954	6	5928
1955	7	5929
1956	8	5930
1957	3	5931
1958	4	5932
1959	5	5933
1960	13	5934
1961	1	5935
1962	2	5936
1963	3	5937
1964	11	5938
1965	6	5939
1966	7	5940
1967	1	5941
1968	9	5942
1969	4	5943
1970	5	5944
1971	6	5945
1972	14	5946
1973	2	5947
1974	3	5948
1975	4	5949
1976	12	5950
1977	7	5951
1978	1	5952
JUBILEE YEAR		
1979	2	5953
1980	10	5954
1981	5	5955
1982	6	5956
1983	7	5957
1984	8	5958
1985	3	5959
1986	4	5960
1987	5	5961
1988	13	5962
1989	1	5963
1990	2	5964
1991	3	5965
1992	11	5966
1993	6	5967
1994	7	5968
1995	1	5969
1996	9	5970
1997	4	5971
1998	5	5972
1999	6	5973
2000	14	5974
2001	2	5975
2002	3	5976
2003	4	5977
2004	12	5978
2005	7	5979
2006	1	5980
2007	2	5981
2008	10	5982
2009	5	5983
2010	6	5984
2011	7	5985
2012	8	5986
2013	3	5987
2014	4	5988
2015	5	5989
2016	13	5990
2017	1	5991
2018	2	5992
2019	3	5993
2020	11	5994
2021	6	5995
2022	7	5996
2033	1	5997
2024	9	5998
2025	4	5999
2026	5	6000
2027	6	6001
2028	14	6002
JUBILEE YEAR		
2029	2	6003
2030	3	6004
2031	4	6005
2032	12	6006
2033	7	6007

THE FOURTEEN POSSIBLE CALENDAR YEARS. NUMBERS 8 THRU 14 ARE ALWAYS LEAP YEARS.

PENTECOST SUNDAYS
ARE CIRCLED IN RED
(SEE FEASTS OF THE LORD PAGE 23)